PRAISE for Don Silver's
A Parent's Guide to Wills & Trusts

Jane Bryant Quinn put *A Parent's Guide to Wills & Trusts* by Don Silver on her holiday gift list in *Woman's Day*.

Excellent book...What also differentiates this book...is the writing itself. It is clear. It is concise. It is clever.
— *LOS ANGELES TIMES*

This [book] is different: it's concisely written, uses simple language and features an easy-to-understand format.
— *CHICAGO SUN-TIMES*

Conversational and easy to understand, Silver uses wit, honesty and brevity (really!) to help parents figure out the best way to address problems.
— *SOUTH FLORIDA PARENTING*

This isn't just another probate/estate book. Tips on avoiding family disputes, considering tax impact and dealing with special circumstances, such as divorce, second marriages and special beneficiaries are remarkably specific and contain details no other general will book offers. *A Parent's Guide to Wills & Trusts* is *must* reading for all parents!
— *WISCONSIN BOOKWATCH*

D0317809

The GENERATION X Money Book

Achieving Security and Independence

The GENERATION X Money Book

Achieving **Security** and Independence

Don Silver

Adams-Hall Publishing
Los Angeles

Requests for such permissions should be addressed to:

Adams-Hall Publishing, PO Box 491002
Los Angeles, CA 90049-1002

No patent liability is assumed with respect to the use of the information contained herein. While every precaution has been taken in the preparation of this book, the publisher and the author assume no responsibility for errors or omissions. Neither is any liability assumed for damages resulting from the use of the information contained herein. This book is intended to provide accurate information. It is not intended, however, to render any legal, tax, accounting, financial, or other professional advice or services. You should therefore use this book as a general guide only. In addition, this book contains information that was available only up to the time of printing.

Although there are certain steps described in this book that you can take yourself, this book is not intended to be a substitute for the professional assistance of an attorney, accountant, financial planner, and life insurance agent. Laws do change with some frequency. That's why you must discuss your situation with qualified professionals before relying solely on the information you may find here or anywhere else.

Assume that all products, company names and Web sites listed in the index and the book are trademarks and/or registered trademarks.

Library of Congress Cataloging-in-Publication Data

Silver, Don
The Generation X Money Book: achieving security and independence
        p.   cm.
    Includes index.
    ISBN 0-944708-30-7 (pbk. : alk paper)

1. Generation X--United States-—Finance, Personal. 2. Finance, Personal--United States. 3. Financial security. I. Title.
HG179.S4743 1998
332.024—dc 21   97-45622
                                                                    CIP

Cover Design by Hespenheide Design (805/373-7336)

Printed in the United States of America
20 19 18 17 16 15 14 13 12 11 10 9 8 7 6 5 4 3 2
First printing 1998

Contents

MOVING TO GREENER PASTURES

LOOKING OUT FOR YOUR PARENTS

TYING OR RETYING THE KNOT

KIDS, STEP-KIDS AND COLLEGE

INSURING YOUR FUTURE

Contents

WILLS & TRUSTS

MAKING MONEY FROM YOUR PAPERWORK

Appendix

Index

Introduction

If you're one of the 40 million people born between 1965 and 1976, you've grown up in an uncertain economy, with job insecurity and the fear that you may foot the bill for others to benefit from Social Security and Medicare.

During your lifetime, as a member of "Generation X," you'll need to maneuver in a marketplace where you may go through seven to ten jobs and up to five different careers. Although you take work seriously, you want a life outside of work that's fun and rewarding.

You want security, independence and a balanced lifestyle. A key to achieving these goals is having enough money, now and in the future.

More so than any generation before you, you need to know how to protect your financial future and be aware in advance of the financial impact of any life-changing decision such as moving to a new job or state or entering into a new marriage.

Traditional money and retirement planning techniques won't work for your generation because you are and will be encountering dramatically new definitions of jobs, work and career, not to mention retirement plans.

This step-by-step, easy-to-read guide is designed to give tips, techniques and evolving money management and lifestyle solutions to use in the 21st Century to give you security and independence.

BUILDING A GOLDEN NEST EGG

1.

Building a nest egg from scratch, starting with the power of a piggy bank

There are three key ways to build a nest egg for your security and independence:

1. Start saving now, no matter how small the amount.
2. Whenever you have a choice, avoid buying on credit.
3. Cut back a little bit on the extras in your life.

If you follow these three steps, you'll be way ahead of your peers.

Don't laugh if your piggy bank makes you rich

It's painless to take your change each day and put it in a piggy bank or even a jar. It's a simple step well worth taking.

The following example illustrates the financial power of piggy banks. Assume, starting at age 23, each evening you put that day's loose change in a piggy bank. If, on the average, you feed piggy 50¢ a day and also throw in an extra dollar bill, at the end of every three months, you'd have around $150 to invest. You could put this money in a tax-deferred or tax-free retirement plan that would grow income tax free.

If your contributions average a 10% yearly return (which is the average growth for stocks since 1926), then at age 65, you'd have over $200,000 from your piggy bank. Nice piggy.

2.

The trick to finding a pot of gold

The trick to accumulating wealth is *not* to budget for it. If you try to budget a share for savings, this item will always be at the bottom of the list since all other expenditures either have a more immediate, short-term benefit or may (inevitably) prove to be more urgent. Instead, you need to make the saving process so automatic that it doesn't require a conscious decision or act by you.

Automatic withdrawals from your paycheck or your checking account that go directly to an IRA, other retirement plan account or into personal savings and investments can achieve this result.

The sooner you set up an *automatic savings plan*, the more you'll have saved up. A simple example shows the benefit of starting to save today.

Scenario One

At age 30, you put $2,000 into an IRA or other *tax-deferred* retirement plan (i.e., one that grows income-tax free until distributions are taken out). At ages 31 and 32, you also add $2,000 each year. Then, you stop making any contributions. If those three $2,000 contributions generate a return of 10% per year, then at age 65 you will have $140,000.

That's $140,000 from three $2,000 contributions.

Scenario Two

If, instead, you waited until age 45 to make your first $2,000 contribution and then you made $2,000 contributions religiously every year for the next 19 years under the same conditions as Scenario One, you would have $114,000, almost 20% less, at age 65.

Compound interest/compound growth

How can 20 contributions of $2,000 produce less than three contributions of $2,000? The answer is *compound interest* (also sometimes called *compound growth*).

Compound interest or compound growth refers to the effect over time of an investment growing in value *and* the reinvested growth also increasing over time. With a savings account, compound interest lets you receive interest on your interest. The longer you've invested, the greater the opportunity for compound interest or growth.

Compound interest is the reason why the earlier you start saving for your financial independence, retirement or your children's college education, the less you'll have to put away each month. With compound interest, once you've worked for your money, your money starts working for you.

The bottom line

Ideally, you should arrange for automatic monthly payments to come off the top and go into some form of investment, inside or outside of an IRA or retirement plan. If that isn't possible due to ever increasing financial demands, then whenever you get a bonus, raise or refund, why not take all or a portion of that windfall to open up or add to your savings, investments or retirement fund?

So what's the lesson? Take the first step and invest as much as you can, as early as you can, to have the greatest opportunity for compound growth. If you delay, you will pay!

3.

A penny saved is not a penny earned

Ben Franklin was only half right when he said "A penny saved is a penny earned." He didn't have to deal with income tax. I wonder what the Boston Tea Party would have been like today if our Founding Fathers had to fill out today's income tax returns.

These days, if you earn two additional dollars on top of your regular income, you may only have about one dollar left after federal and state income tax and Social Security and Medicare taxes.

All of this is leading to how to find the raw material to mold your pot of gold—by prioritizing your money.

Prioritize your money

You need to prioritize your monthly investments among general savings and investments, housing downpayment savings, retirement planning, educational expenses and high-interest, non-deductible debt. Your best investment may be to pay off debt first since you may not find an investment that pays as much as your debt costs you. And the bonus to this strategy is that less debt means less stress.

The best way to learn how to prioritize your money is to carry around a small notebook for one month and write down every single penny you spend. You'll be amazed at where your money goes and how you'll discover painless ways to save money each day.

If you can't earn additional income, the only way left for you to accumulate wealth is to cut expenses. Become a saver.

The "36% return" on your investment

You may have debt on which interest is not deductible (such as personal credit card interest). If you are paying 18% interest on unpaid balances, do you need to earn 36% on your investments or earn the equivalent wages to wind up with the money to pay the 18% interest? It will depend on your income tax bracket. The bottom line is no matter what income tax bracket you are in, you are paying off credit card interest with after-tax, non-deductible dollars.

You may also want to shop around for another credit card with a lower interest rate. Before you switch, make sure you understand whether the lower rate is only for a limited time period. If so, you might get stuck with a much higher rate after the introductory lower rate period. Also, if you are counting on the lower rate applying to prior charges that are being transferred over to a new card, make sure that this indeed is the case. Otherwise, the new rate may only apply to new charges. Pay as much as you can each month to reduce the amount owed as well as the accompanying tension.

If you're a homeowner, it may be wiser to take out a home equity loan to pay off credit card debts so the interest portion of your payments qualifies for an income tax deduction (check with your tax advisor since not all home equity loans qualify for this deduction).

Before seeing a home equity loan as a cure-all, remember, that if you default on a home equity loan, you may lose your house.

You may also want to consider refinancing the loan on your house to lower your monthly payments. Before taking this step, make sure that you consider (1) the costs vs. the benefits especially if you'll want or have to sell your house within a few years of the refinancing and (2) whether you are adding additional years for the payback of your loan. Also see pages 53 and 54 for other possible consequences of a refinancing.

If your debt is over your head

If you want to reduce your debt or become better educated about avoiding debt, consider contacting the National Foundation for Consumer Credit (1/800/388-2227). This network of non-profit organizations offers debt and budget counseling and debt repayment programs. Their services are either at no cost or a low cost.

Bottom line

Remember, saving money is a great way to make money! It beats working for it. If you have flexible benefits at work that expire at the end of the year, keep an eye on the available benefits so they are not wasted.

Even one-time steps can pay off big. If, at age 25, you spent $2,000 less than you planned on a car and invested that $2,000 in a Roth IRA (see pages 16-19), you could have $50,000 in tax-free dollars at age 65.

Also look at small ways you can save every day or at least once a week: brown-bagging your lunch, clipping some coupons or renting a movie instead of going out. Even these small steps can add up to hundreds of thousands of dollars over a working lifetime through the power of compound growth.

4.

When to start and how much to put into your golden nest egg

To achieve security and independence, you need to start building your nest egg now. Time is on your side, but not forever. Next to money, time is your best ally. The earlier you start, the less risk you have to take in investing since there's more time for compound growth. Also, you will be in a better position to ride out the inevitable highs and lows in the economy and your career.

Every little bit you save now will grow and multiply over the years due to compound growth. Every year you delay getting started will cost you more than you can imagine. If you are age 25 and you delay for one year in setting up a Roth IRA (see pages 16-19), you may have nearly $50,000 less at age 65. If you delay for five years, you may have $200,000 less at age 65.

Getting started

Saving is a habit. If you start saving, you'll be hooked for life.

A one-year savings plan

Once you've got your debt under control (see pages 9 to 11), it's time to take the first saving step. Aim low and try to save 1% of your income in the first month. If you earn $2,000 per month, try to save $20 (the piggy bank technique on page 5 should make this easy to do.

The next month, try to save 2% of your income ($40 in this example). For the next three months, increase your percentage by 1% per month (3% or $60, in the third month, 4% or $80 in the fourth month and 5% or $100 in the fifth month with this $2,000 per month example). If you miss your goal one month, try to reach it the next month.

Try to keep up the 5% per month saving schedule for the next seven months to complete the year.

Don't get discouraged if you can't save 5% every month. Remember, if you miss your goal one month, try to reach it the next month.

The year-two savings plan

You can stay at this 5% level for a couple of years or, if you're really serious about protecting your future, read on for year two.

If all goes well, then, in year two, try to save 1% more each month for the first five months (6% in the first month, 7% in the second month, 8% in the third month, 9% in the third month and 10% in the fourth month). Then, stay at the 10% level for the next few years unless you can put even more away.

Again, if you can't reach the 10% goal, do the best you can. The idea is to develop the saving habit and maximize your savings while you're young. That way, compound growth will do a lot of the work for you over time to build your golden nest egg.

How to calculate the right-size nest egg

As time goes by, you'll want to select a financial advisor (see pages 35-37) to help you pinpoint the ideal size of your nest egg and the monthly savings amount to build the nest egg.

When you see financial calculations, you need to know what's behind the numbers.

Every financial projection is a series of assumptions. A small change in an assumption such as the future rate of return (growth) or the inflation rate can have dramatic effects. Whenever you review a financial projection, ask the preparer of the data whether the preparer used "optimistic," "pessimistic" or "realistic" assumptions. Always ask to see separate calculations based on these three types of assumptions.

Effect of an inheritance

You may think "I don't need to save. I'll ultimately inherit quite a bit from my parents." However, you don't know:

1. What financial roadblocks may affect the size of that inheritance, including financial reverses suffered by parents and high nursing home or other medical costs for parents.

2. Who will be named as your parent(s)' beneficiaries (if you are married, you and your spouse may be assuming that there will be two inheritances; however, if your spouse passes away before your in-laws, it's quite likely that your spouse's parents will not include you in their will or trust).

3. What death tax costs will be at that time.

Computer programs and on-line information

See the Appendix on pages 152 and 153 for computer programs and Web sites with on-line calculators.

5.

How to keep your pot of gold

If you don't learn a few income tax rules, you'll pay unnecessary taxes and lose some of the power to control your financial destiny. In some cases on your investments, you can
(a) choose to incur higher taxes, lower taxes or no taxes and
(b) decide when you pay the income tax. Each choice has a
benefit and a downside.

Why learn about saving income tax? It's only important if you
want to achieve financial independence and security and want
to have flexibility as to your career and lifestyle choices, now
and down the road.

The higher tax and the lower tax

There are two main types of income tax: *ordinary income tax*
and *capital gains tax*. There's one special kind of capital gains
tax known as *long-term capital gain tax*.

The ordinary income tax rate is higher (15% to 39.6% federal
rate) than the long-term capital gains tax rate (8% to 20%
federal rate for certain investments). These are the higher tax
and lower tax options mentioned above.

Ordinary income tax applies to income such as your wages,
interest and dividends. Long-term capital gains tax applies to
the gain when investments such as stocks or mutual funds are
sold that have been held for a long enough period of time.
Mutual funds are companies with professional managers that
pool your money with that of other investors to buy stocks
and/or bonds.

The long-term capital gains tax rate is lower than the ordinary income tax rate. That's not the end of the story. Some investments are tax-deferred (i.e., payment of the tax is delayed) and some are tax-free (no income tax is due).

Tax-deferred investments

A tax-deferred investment is one that isn't reduced by income tax while it is growing (income tax is paid later when distributions are taken out). It's no mystery why a tax-deferred investment grows faster than a non-deferred one. If the IRS suddenly announced you didn't have to pay income tax, your paycheck or profit would go up and you would have more money. An example of a tax-deferred investment is the *traditional individual retirement account* ("IRA"). This type of IRA may get you a tax-deduction for each IRA contribution but it is subject to ordinary income tax (15% to 39.6% federal rate) when distributions are taken out.

Tax-free investment possibility

The 1997 tax act introduced a new kind of savings vehicle, the *Roth IRA*. With a Roth IRA, the tax benefit comes at the end. Withdrawals (including the contributions and the growth over the years) may be income tax-free. The contributions are not tax-deductible. The Roth IRA may not just defer (delay) income tax. If all the requirements are met, the Roth IRA can be federal income tax free. This is the no-tax option. Since the Roth IRA requirements may change over time as to who is eligible to make a contribution and how long your money must be kept in the IRA, you should always check with your tax advisor before making a contribution or a withdrawal.

At the time this book is being written, you can withdraw your Roth IRA contributions (but not the growth or earnings) at any time without the 10% penalty or income tax being due (withdrawals are considered to come first from your contributions). Always check with your tax advisor before making a contribution or a withdrawal since the rules may change over time.

The option of withdrawing contributions without incurring income tax can make the Roth IRA a very flexible investment tool. That flexibility, combined with possible income tax-free growth, makes a Roth IRA a valuable investment.

What's better for you—a traditional IRA or a Roth IRA?

You'll probably want the Roth IRA. It makes more sense to use a Roth IRA with these four factors: (a) the younger you are, (b) the longer you delay taking distributions from the IRA, (c) the lower your current income tax bracket and (d) the higher your anticipated income tax bracket in retirement.

Distributions of growth from both types of IRA before age 59½ are subject to income tax and may also cause a 10% penalty (unless an exception applies). Distributions of your contributions from a traditional IRA before age 59½ fall under the same rules but distributions of your contributions from a Roth IRA are different. At the time this book is being written, you can withdraw your Roth IRA contributions (but not the growth or earnings) at any time without the 10% penalty or income tax being due (withdrawals are considered to come first from your contributions).

The first step in deciding between the IRAs is to check the eligibility requirements for each IRA. Then, you need to compare the current and future tax benefits of the "maybe get a deduction now but pay ordinary income tax later traditional IRA" vs. the "don't deduct now, probably get income-tax free money later Roth IRA." Your financial advisor and/or CPA has to run the numbers and look at the state income tax rules for your situation. To help you decide which kind of IRA is best for you, you may want to use the Vanguard IRA Worksheet on their Internet Web site (http://www.vanguard.com).

Traditional IRAs require distributions to begin at age 70½. Roth IRAs are not subject to this requirement so they can grow income tax-free, possibly for generations.

The Roth IRA rollover

Traditional IRAs may be rolled over into the new Roth IRA if all the requirements are met. The rollover will generate a tax at the time of rollover (which if made in 1998, may be spread out over four years) but then allow the remaining amount and all of the future growth to be paid out federal income tax free (if all the requirements are met). Consult with your accountant to see if this rollover makes sense for your particular situation and to determine where the funds will come from to pay the rollover tax (you probably won't want to dip into the Roth IRA to pay the rollover tax). Also, before withdrawing any funds from a qualified retirement plan as the first step in completing a traditional IRA to Roth IRA transfer, make sure the retirement plan is up-to-date and fully qualified to avoid an income tax surprise.

Why you may want to make taxable, long-term capital gains-type investments

If you want flexibility to use your money any time you want, any way you want, then any kind of IRA may not the best place for you (at least not for all of your money). Instead, you'll want to investigate investing in stocks and mutual funds in your personal name (outside of any IRA or retirement plan) and holding investments long enough to qualify for the long-term capital gains tax (8% to 20% federal rate).

One long-term planning benefit of capital gains-type assets should be mentioned here. A sale of assets held in your personal name while you are alive may cause more or less income tax than a sale after your death. Ask your accountant about the income-tax basis rules when there is a death.

Here's an example of how these income tax rules could apply way down the road. Assume you are very ill and are considering selling assets held in your personal name (and outside any IRA or retirement plan) to make things simpler for your heirs. There could be a tremendous amount of pent-up capital gain in your assets (e.g., a stock you paid $50,000 for is now worth $200,000). If you sell now, there is income tax to pay on the gain. If, instead, your heirs inherit the assets and they sell the assets, their starting point for federal income tax gain or loss is what the assets were worth on the date of your death ($200,000 in this example). For investments that have gone down in value, you might take the opposite approach and sell during your lifetime. Check with your accountant since the difference can amount to tens or hundreds of thousands of dollars in unnecessary income tax. Remember, however, the rules with retirement plan assets can be different.

Why you may want to avoid investments in your personal name

If you have mutual funds in your personal name, they pay out almost of all of their income each year to the holders of the funds.

Some funds have larger gains than others that will have to come out sometime (and be taxable to you even if you haven't sold the fund). Since that's taxable income to the fundholder (you) including interest, dividends and short and long-term capital gains, find out before you invest in a fund how much pent-up profit trouble could come bursting into your bubble even if the growth occurred before you became involved with the fund. Even if this income is automatically reinvested for you in the fund, it's taxable income for the fundholder (you) that year unless the mutual fund is in a tax-deferred plan such as a traditional IRA (or a potentially tax-free Roth IRA). The bottom line is that you may need to shell out big bucks in income tax for gains you are reinvesting and not putting into your pocket that year.

If you tend to buy and hold stocks and mutual funds for a long period of time, you might want these investments held in your personal name, rather than in an IRA or other retirement plan. This could entitle you to favorable federal long-term capital gains income tax (a federal income tax of 8% to 20% on the gain) as compared to the income tax on a traditional IRA/retirement plan distribution (up to a federal "ordinary" income tax of 39.6%). Some retirement plan distributions qualify for special income-tax averaging rates. Ask your accountant about the best way for you to receive distributions.

Likewise, you'll want to consider having mutual funds owned in your personal name that generate more long-term capital gains tax as compared to ordinary income tax. Be sure to ask how "tax efficient" a mutual fund is and its rate of turnover (how quickly a fund sells its investments to determine how much you'll owe each year in long-term capital gains tax or ordinary income tax on assets held in your personal name). Stay on top of this issue because the turnover rate in the past may not be the turnover rate in the future.

If there is a lot of change in your investments, you might want to hold assets inside a 401(k), IRA or other retirement plan since no income tax is paid until distributions are made. And, with a Roth IRA, there may not be any income tax due (see pages 16-19).

The rule of thumb is to have high turnover rates in tax-deferred and tax-free accounts and low turnover rates in your individual name accounts.

Your best bet is to talk to an accountant to see how much you'll benefit from each option and whether you'll qualify to take advantage of each option.

6.

401(k) plan do's and don'ts

If you have a retirement plan at work, chances are it's a 401(k) plan. A 401(k) plans delays income tax until the retirement funds are withdrawn (i.e., it's a tax-deferred investment—see page 16). This allows your nest egg to grow each year without the tax person taking a bite during the growing years.

Here are seven do's and don'ts on your 401(k) plan:

1. *Don't say no to free money*

Although you, the employee, put in the lion's share of the contributions, usually your employer will match at least some of your contribution (up to certain limits).

If your company has one of those "matching" 401(k) plans and you're not participating at all or not participating to the fullest extent possible, you're giving up free money. Over the long-haul, you could be passing up tens or hundreds of thousands of dollars including the growth of employer contributions.

Once you reach the matching limit of your employer, you might want to consider making a contribution to a Roth IRA (see pages 16-19) with your next available funds to try to qualify for tax-free income. Then, if you still have some money leftover and your 401(k) allows an additional contribution, you could make another contribution to the 401(k) plan.

2. Your 401(k) is not an ATM window

You may be able to borrow from your 401(k) for your short-term needs. But this is a retirement fund. If this isn't enough to convince you to resist temptation, remember that when you pay back your 401(k) loan, you're using after-tax money to do so and you may not receive an income tax deduction on the interest you're paying back.

If you leave your job and don't repay your loan before rolling the 401(k) directly over to a new employer or IRA custodian, you've just received a taxable distribution. See if your plan requires the repayment of the loan, too.

Remember, the idea is make your 401(k) a tax-advantaged vehicle, not a tax cow for the government.

3. Avoid early withdrawals that incur penalties

If you're not careful, early withdrawals will cause you to owe income tax on the withdrawn amount plus a 10% federal penalty. Try to rollover any distribution amounts without having them touched by you.

4. Mix and match your 401(k) investments

Make sure your retirement plan is not too top-heavy in any one company or industry. Balance risk with growth opportunities and how much time you have until retirement age to recoup any unfortunate investment decisions. The more time you have to recover, the more risk you can afford to take.

5. Changing jobs and dealing with your 401(k) can be complicated

If you had a 401(k) at your old job, you may be able to leave the money there, cash it in, transfer it a new employer's 401(k) plan or, in some cases, roll it over to an IRA.

You may want to leave your retirement account in your former employer's retirement plan. If you leave the company, withdraw your retirement account and later return to work for the same (or related) company, you may not receive credit under the retirement plan for your first work stay. Take a look at the company's Summary Plan Description (see pages 25 and 26) and obtain advice before taking a distribution.

If you roll it over to an IRA, don't count on being able to put it back into another 401(k) unless you rolled it into a special IRA known as a conduit IRA. Ask your accountant about the details.

6. *See if you can control who inherits the 401(k) if you die before your spouse*

Ask your attorney whether you can make sure who inherits your 401(k) or your spouse's 401(k) if you die before your spouse. Also, discuss whether you want your surviving spouse to be able to change the ultimate beneficiary after your death due to unforeseen circumstances that may occur down the road.

7. *401(k) investments require your attention*

At least once a year, look with your accountant or financial advisor at how your 401(k) investments are doing and whether they're meeting your long-term goals. With the federal income tax rules, you generally want (i) high dividend and interest paying investments inside your 401(k) and (ii) growth, capital gain type investments outside your 401(k) to minimize the ultimate income tax bite. Your accountant can advise you as to what is best for your particular situation.

7.

Honey, they shrunk the pension!

Don't overlook the possibility of mistakes occurring in your company's retirement plan (or your own plan if you are self-employed). Even small errors can grow to significant dollar losses for you since the effects will compound over the years.

As the years go by, how will you be able to find and correct a mistake made in the prior century? The answer is, you won't, so monitor your plan each year.

Some surprises are turning up in retirement plans

Just when retirement plans are growing in size and importance, some surprises are turning up in retirement plan distributions.

The latest government audit discovered that more than 13% of participants in defined benefit pension plans (where the employer provides the funding and the retirement benefit is a fixed percentage of an employee's earnings) were being underpaid.

It appears at this time that the underpayments were unintentional. Most mistakes have resulted from one or more of the following factors: defective software, errors in inputting earnings, length of employment and life expectancies as well as just the complexity of pension laws.

Some of these mistakes could have been prevented if employees double-checked their employer's records each year. However, in many cases, it takes a pension expert playing detective to uncover the shortages. It may be worth it for you to call the National Center for Retirement Benefits, Inc. ("NCRB"). The NCRB pays for all of the expenses of investigation and it receives a fee only from the benefits recovered for you. The NCRB does not handle governmental or union/multi-employer plans. If you call the NCRB (1/800/666-1000), you can receive a free brochure and a list of 30 serious errors and problems found in pension and profit sharing plans.

Steps to take now

Don't wait for Congress to reform the retirement plan laws before taking the following steps:

• First, get a Summary Plan Description ("SPD") from your employer that tells you how retirement benefits are calculated and paid out. Read the description and ask questions until you really understand it.

• Before changing jobs and giving up your current retirement plan benefits, look at the new company's SPD to see what's in store for you.

• When reviewing the SPD (and annual statements from your employer), look to see:

(1) whether retirement plan benefits are determined just from your base salary or whether bonuses, overtime and commissions are also included;

(2) whether your employer will match all, part, or none of the contributions made by you to the company's 401(k) plan;

(3) what the limit is for contributions by you to the company plan;

(4) whether employer contributions each year are based on a percentage of your salary that year or determined by a formula that also considers your age and the number of years you have until retirement;

(5) whether retirement benefits (in the case of certain pension plans) are based on just your highest-earning years (no matter when they occurred in your employment career);

(6) whether your time worked at companies co-owned or part of the same family of companies is counted;

(7) how years of service are calculated if you take a pregnancy break or some other leave of absence (or even another job) and then come back (You may want to leave your retirement account in your former employer's retirement plan. If you leave the company, withdraw your retirement account and later return to work for the same (or related) company, you may not receive credit under the retirement plan for your first work stay. Take a look at the company's Summary Plan Description and obtain advice before taking a distribution); and

(8) whether your pension is reduced by a portion or all of your Social Security retirement benefit (this is commonly called "Social Security integration").

• Call or write your Senators and Congressional represent-ative and ask them to simplify the pension laws to help eliminate underpayments.

It could be a long wait until you receive your pension benefits

It's not bad enough that you might be shortchanged on your retirement benefits. It could be worse. You could have to wait decades for the underpayments to begin.

Imagine, that you left your employer when you were age 35. You're sitting by the mailbox waiting for the payout of your retirement plan benefits so you can pay the bills until you find your next job. You may have a long wait. This is another reason to take control of your financial future and have investments in your personal name (and outside of any IRA and retirement plan).

In many cases, employers can legally wait until you reach age 65 to distribute your retirement benefits. It doesn't matter that you need your vested benefits paid to you in 30 days, not 30 years. Again, take a look at your plan's Summary Plan Description to see what your employer is required to do on distributions. The good news is that many employers make lump-sum distributions in a matter of months, not years.

Before a retirement plan distribution is made, it's always a good idea to first get tax advice as to the income tax consequences of the different distribution choices and how to handle loans taken against your retirement benefits.

For many of us, our employer's retirement plan may be more important in the long-run than Social Security benefits. Be vigilant and take the time to become educated. When you receive your employer's retirement plan statement each year, double check it. Surprises can be fun but not usually with retirement distributions.

8.

Preventing Social InSecurity

There are three sources you may be able to draw upon for retirement income: (1) your company's retirement plan, (2) your personal savings and investments, and (3) Social Security.

When planning for your future, it would probably be a safe guess that Congress will eventually increase the full retirement age from age 67 (it's not age 65 for your generation) for you to at least age 70 (and probably age 72) to help keep down the cost of Social Security benefits.

Why you should care about Social Security right now

When you think of Social Security, you usually just think of retirement benefits. But Social Security may also provide an additional package of benefits to you and your family *right now* if you become severely disabled before retirement age or to your family upon your death. Social Security can thus provide an important base of *disability,* and *survivors* benefits for you *and* your family; however, don't rely solely on it.

Benefits could be hundreds of thousands of dollars

Most people underestimate the potential size of these benefits. The benefits could be worth hundreds of thousands of dollars to you and your loved ones.

For example, if you passed away in 1997, leaving a spouse and two young children (ages four and two), and your family currently could receive up to $30,000 per year for many years. Over the years, the family benefits could amount to hundreds of thousands of dollars. (If you want to see typical retirement, disability and survivor benefits, take a look at the tables on pages 149 and 150 in the Appendix.)

To avoid being shortchanged, you need to make sure Social Security has recorded your earnings correctly since it is *earnings* that determine the benefit amounts for you and certain family members.

When you or your family members apply for any of these possible Social Security benefits, how will you or they know if the benefits are based on the correct amount of your earnings? There is a simple way to find out and it costs one stamp every three years.

Form SSA-7004

To keep an eye on the information being used by Social Security, you need to complete a *Request for Earnings and Benefit Estimate Statement* (Form SSA-7004) at least every three years.

The form is free and it's easy to obtain (call 1/800-772-1213 to order the form). Then you just fill out the simple form and mail it to the Social Security Administration.

Social Security will mail a listing of your earnings (according to their records) and a projection of your Social Security retirement, disability and survivors benefits. You just need to compare one or two lines of your income tax returns with the benefit statement to determine whether the Social Security records are accurate. If there is any mistake in their records, you should have it corrected before it's too late.

How you can be shortchanged

Social Security has to deal with the earnings of every working person in the country every year. Do you think it's possible when keying in information for more than 130 million workers that a data entry operator ever leaves off a digit (thus changing $31,000 to $3,100) or reverses digits (changing $31,000 to $13,000)? It just may be your luck that you'll be the one this happens to. Even if Social Security never makes a mistake, could your company make one in sending in your earnings record?

The name is the game

Have you always filled in your payroll forms exactly the same way or have you sometimes used a full middle name and other times just an initial? The safest way is to always match the name on your Social Security card identically to that on employment forms, including W-2 forms.

And, if you're a woman who has married and/or divorced and changed her name, have you advised Social Security of all name changes?

No problem, you say, since when the time rolls around to collect benefits, you'll double check everything. That's what you say. There are two problems with this reasoning.

First, in the year 2040 you probably won't be able to *find* your tax returns to verify your earnings from the 1990s. Second, and more important, even if you could locate those records, it could be too late under the law to make Social Security correct its records. The law makes it your responsibility to be sure Social Security records your earnings correctly. There are time limits for correcting errors. You may lose tremendous benefits for the rest of your life (and reduce your family's benefits, too) if a mistake is reported too late.

On-line information

Go to the Social Security Website (http://www.ssa.gov) and look up a wealth of information including explanations, publications and examples.

9.

Avoiding ten common errors

You may prevent a ten mistakes that frequently occur in planning a financial future by taking the following steps:

1. First, determine your goals and objectives. How important is it for you to own a house right now as compared to your other goals? Since there is never enough money to satisfy all our needs and desires, you need to know what's most important to you, now and in the long run.

2. Maximize contributions to *tax-deferred* retirement plans where your employer matches at least part of your contribution (see page 16).

3. Diversify investments (don't put all of your nest eggs in the same basket).

   Usually, it's not a good idea to buy just a few stocks, or invest in just one mutual fund—it's too easy for your entire financial future to go sour this way. Even if you invest in different mutual funds, see if the investing philosophy differs among the funds otherwise you might really be putting nearly one identical nest egg on top of another instead of spreading the risk around the hen-house.

   Take the time and effort to monitor how your investments are doing (even if you have a financial advisor).

4. Consider the effect of inflation.

Even though no one can predict the future, we usually look to the past in trying to decide what inflation (increases in the cost-of-living), interest rates and rates of return on investments will be like down the road. We get a certain comfort in knowing history, including financial history, which helps us make educated guesses about the future.

The Great Depression started in 1929. If you look at investment returns since 1926, three years before the start of the Depression, there are some interesting results.

During the more than 70 years since 1926, stocks have averaged a compounded annual return of about 10%. During the same period, long-term interest rates and bonds have averaged about half of that.

Within any given year as well as any 10-year period, each of these types of investments has often suffered tremendous losses as well as enjoyed startling gains.

Every financial projection for retirement benefits and education costs in this book (and outside of it) is just an estimate but is based on observations about the past.

Effect of inflation

Inflation has averaged 4% over the last 40 years. Over the last 25 years, it has averaged almost 6%.

If inflation (i.e., the cost of living) goes up 4% per year, after 18 years, a dollar is worth just 50¢. After 36 years of 4% per year inflation, a dollar is worth just 25¢.

THE GENERATION X MONEY BOOK

5. Assess your risk comfort level.

   Take a peek at the worst-case scenario for each alternative. When you review alternative investment choices, pretend you've made the investments before you actually do so. Take a piece of paper and cut it up into smaller pieces each labelled with the type of investment and dollar amount of each investment. Put the papers under your pillow and see how you sleep the next week. If you're a nervous wreck from make-believe investments, just imagine how the real thing will affect you).

6. Avoid a risky investment that promises too big a profit.

   Before you make an investment, get professional advice and understand what the cost will be to get out of it if you conclude the investment was a mistake.

7. Select your financial advisor very carefully.

   As your nest egg grows, have an annual financial checkup with a qualified professional to evaluate your goals, your progress, the effect of new laws and new family or financial circumstances.

8. Start saving as soon as possible.

9. Get professional advice before moving your retirement assets when you leave your job. Different approaches can cost or save you hundreds of thousands of dollars.

10. Consider the effects of income taxes, including state taxes and taxes due on early withdrawals of investments. Consider non-tax costs of investments (e.g., high fees if you want to bail out early from an annuity; lack of liquidity so that it's difficult to get your money out of a limited partnership; or high annual management costs with some mutual funds).

10.

How to select a financial advisor

Will you spend more time thinking about the topping for your next pizza than you will in selecting a financial advisor?

Among the questions you should *ask yourself* are:

1. Does my accountant know and recommend a good financial advisor?

2. Do I know other clients who have worked with the advisor for at least several years?

   Ideally, you would answer "yes" to both of these questions but a "yes" to either one may be sufficient.

3. Have I called the state regulatory agency to see if there are any disciplinary actions against the advisor?

Among the questions you should *ask the prospective advisor* are:

1. Am I like your typical client?

2. What are your qualifications and length of experience?

3. How will you be compensated? Will you earn a fee *(a)* on commissions for selling investments, *(b)* a fee for services but no commissions, or *(c)* a combination of a fee and commissions? Is your fee a flat fee including all services or is it calculated on an hourly basis at a specified hourly rate?

All things being equal, the fee with no commission, option *(b)*, should result in the most objective advice for you.

4. Will you let me see financial plans of other clients like me with the client names blocked out?

The *prospective financial advisor should ask you (and you should be prepared to answer)* at least the following questions:

1. What are your financial and personal goals, short-term and long-term?

2. How much risk are you willing to take on investments?

3. What are your needs for cash besides what is invested in long-term investments?

The *financial advisor should do* at least the following:

1. Fully explain, orally and in writing, a probable game plan for the next year as well as the next 3, 5, 10, and 20 years.

2. Fully explain, orally and in writing, a proposed investment and wait for you to feel comfortable with it before having you plunk down your money.

3. Welcome questions from you and provide easily understood answers.

Where to find a financial advisor

There are a lot of people out there who want to give you financial advice. How can you determine the qualifications of a good financial advisor? A good place to start is to ask your accountant and attorney. You may want someone who has earned the designation of Certified Financial Planner (CFP),

Chartered Financial Consultant (ChFC) or a CPA/Personal Financial Specialist.

And, remember, an advisor recommends investments geared to meeting *your* objectives—not the other way around.

11.

Saving taxes on distributions from retirement plans

Distributions from retirement plans can be subject to income, death and penalty taxes. There are usually ways to minimize the impact of all of these taxes if steps are taken in advance to plan for them.

Avoiding unnecessary income tax

If you aren't careful, you'll pay an unnecessary 20% income tax on a retirement plan distribution you intended to *roll over* (i.e., put into another qualified retirement plan).

This tax very often comes about if your employer is downsizing (or now euphemistically known as "right-sizing") and your retirement benefits are transferred out of your former employer's retirement plan. Your employer might ask you a simple question, "Do you want the money sent directly to you?" and innocently enough you respond, "Sure." You can, in fact, avoid this tax by not touching the retirement plan distribution even for an instant.

Instead, have the distribution go directly into an IRA rollover or another *qualified plan* (see if the new employer's plan allows you to do so from day one on the job).

If, instead, your retirement plan benefits are distributed directly to you and you, in turn, immediately put the distribution into an IRA or your new employer's plan, the IRS requires 20% of the distribution to be withheld from you (and paid to the IRS). In addition to this 20% withholding, you may have to pay income tax on the withheld portion (plus a 10% penalty if you are under age 59½). Always get professional advice before retirement benefits are distributed.

Company stock

In certain cases, you may get favorable capital gain treatment by *not* rolling company stock from a retirement plan into an IRA. You and your heirs may be income tax and estate tax dollars ahead in the long run by instead putting the stock into your individual name. Although there will be some income tax due right away by doing this, have your accountant run the numbers to see how beneficial this technique might be in your case.

Also, if your employee benefits include income tax-favored options to purchase stock, ask your accountant how the capital gains tax and alternative minimum tax will affect you.

Beneficiary designations. Talk to your accountant and attorney about how you should complete your beneficiary designation forms to save and/or defer income and death taxes on retirement plan distributions. In some cases, distributions can even be stretched out over time for your children so that they can have a tax-deferred nest-egg growing over decades.

Taking money out early

Generally, early withdrawals (before age 59½) from retirement plans and IRAs are subject to a penalty besides income tax. However, if you need to take money out of a retirement plan before age 59½, ask your accountant whether you fit under one of the exceptions.

12.

The federally insured surprise: retirement assets in banks may not be fully federally insured

You probably know that mutual funds are *not* federally insured. When you invest in a mutual fund, you are depending upon your common sense and governmental regulators to be sure any given fund is kept in line.

However, you may think that *all* retirement funds in banks are *completely* federally insured. Not so. The maximum federal insurance limit on bank deposits for IRAs, Keogh plans, and 401(k) plans is currently $100,000. That's $100,000 total per bank and not $100,000 per type of plan.

Whether you have one or more of these types of plans, you should always confirm the Federal Deposit Insurance Corporation limit for your funds in bank accounts. The solution currently is to keep under the $100,000 FDIC limit in any one institution.

Even if you do not have $100,000 in retirement funds in a bank now, you might in the future. And even if you will never have $100,000 in such plans, you still could be affected if the regulations lower the insured limit in the future. There are also rules on the $100,000 limitation for non-retirement accounts, too. So, at least every year, have your banker confirm the federally insured limits for your retirement plans and other accounts at the bank.

13.

Protecting retirement plan assets

There are four main ways you can protect retirement plan assets. Three of the techniques protect you and one protects your heirs.

First, be diligent concerning the investment of retirement plan assets. More and more you'll see fraudulent, pie-in-the-sky schemes to lure retirement investors.

Second, become aware of the tax rules on different types of distributions and how beneficiary designations can affect the deferral of income tax.

Third, if you own a business, be aware that different types of retirement plans offer different degrees of protection in case you ever need to file bankruptcy. With some types of plans, you may be able to keep the retirement plan assets from going to creditors as part of a bankruptcy. With other types of plans, the retirement plan assets could be totally lost. You should talk to your attorney about the possibilities for your situation.

Fourth, ask your attorney how to complete beneficiary designations to prevent retirement plan assets from going through probate unnecessarily if you die. Probate would result in higher attorney's fees and assets possibly going to creditors instead of your family (see page 138).

14.

What the future holds

During your lifetime, you will probably see all of the following:

- The economy go through periods of tremendous growth and prosperity, recession and depression

- The income tax, death tax and Social Security tax laws undergo tremendous change

- Social Security and Medicare revised to a degree unimaginable in the late 20th Century

- Society changed dramatically as the 77 million Baby Boomers born between 1946 and 1964 begin their retirement journey

- A career with changes that you can't imagine now

- Life expectancies increase so that it's very common to live to age 100.

Your job is to be flexible, aware and knowledgeable to deal with all this change. Be prepared to sacrifice salary to get a better job. Be ready to become educated in new fields and technologies. There's no one right away to build a secure financial future. There are many possible investments out there: stocks, bonds, mutual funds, real estate, annuities, savings accounts, IRAs, 401(k) plans, retirement plans and owning a business. You're an individual and you'll find the financial solutions that are right for you.

MY HOUSE
IS MY CASTLE

15.

To buy or not to buy, that is the question

There are financial and psychological benefits of owning a house.

Tell me the good news

Buying, rather than renting, can result in owning a substantial asset (especially once the loan has been paid off). By making mortgage payments, you are saving. The reason is that once the mortgage is paid off, you own a hopefully, valuable asset that can be sold or just enjoyed. There can be income tax advantages, too. The interest portion of mortgage payments is usually deductible from your income tax (reducing your income tax bill). And, there are special rules on selling a house that may make most or all of the gain income-tax free.

Home sales

Married couples can now avoid federal income tax on up to $500,000 of gain on the sale of their primary residence (also see pages 141 and 142). Single persons can exempt half that amount. Your state's law may be different. If your house was sold before 1998, check with your accountant as to the tax rules applicable to your sale.

In general, there is a two-year ownership period to qualify but there are exceptions for changes in employment, health or certain other unforeseen circumstances that could allow for a partial benefit. The exemption can be used repeatedly as long as the two-year and primary residence requirements are met.

If you're about to get married and trying to save up for a downpayment, you might make wedding guests aware of a Federal Housing Administration (FHA) program. The federal program allows couples to open up savings accounts at FHA approved banks and friends and family can contribute to the downpayment account.

And, the bad news?

Houses can go down in value, even below what you owe on the property. You can lose your entire investment. You have to be careful because in some cases you can be personally liable to pay the mortgage balance even if the house is sold to pay a portion of the balance.

Depending upon how your mortgage is written, you can be subject to early payment penalties if you sell your house before the mortgage is paid off.

And, remember, it's okay to mortgage the house but don't mortgage your future by taking on too large a house loan.

What to do?

In general, if you think you've settled down and you're going to own your home for at least five years, then it's probably a good idea to buy one. However, if your work situation is not stable enough to know that you'll live in the same area, think twice about the selling costs you'll need to pay and what will happen if you can't sell your house when you need to move. Renting, instead of owning, can be a very wise move in many cases.

When you're ready to start looking at houses, first find out what the purchase transaction and home ownership costs will be (be ready to negotiate to save money). Shop for a loan so you get the best deal (consider contacting the National Foundation for Consumer Credit, 1/800/388-2227, for advice on getting the best loan—see page 11). Also see the Web sites in the Appendix on pages 152 and 153.

How reliable you've been in paying your other bills can affect your house mortgage. Good credit risks have a much easier time qualifying for mortgages. Bad credit risks either can't qualify for a loan or will often have to accept a loan with a higher rate of interest. Be aware that your credit worthiness may be downgraded if "too many" creditors have looked at your credit record. Be careful in giving too many authorizations to creditors in shopping for car loans, house loans or other purposes. You may be able to get pre-approved for a loan so you know exactly how expensive a house is affordable for you.

Keep in the back of your mind that the 77 million Baby Boomers will start reaching age 65 in the year 2011. The last of the Boomers will reach age 65 in the year 2029. A lot of these Boomers will want to sell their houses to fund their retirement. Since Baby Boomers outnumber your generation two-to-one, there may be a glut of houses on the market. Only the future will tell.

16.

How to take years off your mortgage payments

If you just bought a house or refinanced it, there is a good chance that you have a mortgage that will take nearly another 30 years to be paid off. How old will you be in 30 years? Do you still want to be making mortgage payments at age 60 or 65?

There are two easy ways to avoid 30 years of mortgage payments. One way is to take out a 15-year loan. With a 15-year loan, you're making higher monthly payments for 15 years (though usually at a lower interest rate, about ½% below the rate on a 30-year loan). This type of loan commits you to higher monthly payments throughout the 15 years.

The advantage of a 15-year loan as compared to a 30-year loan is that the *total interest paid* by you is much *lower* since your loan will be paid off in half the time (compare examples one and four on pages 50 and 51).

Another way to pay your loan off sooner

Another way to save interest, but have greater flexibility as to the amount of your monthly payment, is to have a 30-year loan and make extra payments in an amount you determine. A small but regular extra payment can result in your saving interest payments equal to 50% or more of the original loan amount.

There are two main questions you need to ask yourself in deciding whether to pay off your loan early. First, what is the financial benefit or detriment of paying off your loan early? Second, what is the psychological benefit you'll receive if your home is debt-free at retirement age or earlier?

Financial considerations

If your house is not worth much more than your loan, it may not be a good idea to pay extra money on the loan.

If you do not pay off your mortgage early, you will probably get an income tax benefit from deducting the mortgage interest on your income tax return. This reduces the real cost of your mortgage payments. Have your accountant explain the income tax rules that may limit, however, the actual benefit of mortgage interest deductions, especially with refinanced loans.

If you do not pay off your loan early, you will have more money to invest. But will you invest that money to receive a greater benefit than paying off your loan early?

If you pay off your loan early, will too much of your net worth be tied up in your house, which is an illiquid asset (i.e., hard to turn into cash immediately)?

If you have a 30-year loan, there are three ways to make extra payments to reduce the length (and cost) of your 30-year loan. One way, the hardest way, is to come up with one extra monthly payment each year so that you actually make 13 monthly payments per year instead of 12 payments per year.

A second way that may be available through your lender is to let you make payments every two weeks so you still end up making 13 monthly payments but you do it through 26 bi-weekly payments. The third way is just to pay something extra every month (e.g., $100) with your regular mortgage payment, ideally through an automatic withdrawal from your checking account. That reduces your principal balance by that extra amount ($100) per month.

The following four examples show the effect of various payment schedules and assume that there is a $100,000 fixed-rate loan that is taken out (or refinanced) when you are 30 years old.

Example One: 30-year loan at 8% interest with no extra payments

360 payments (30 years times 12 payments per year) of $734 each for a total of **$264,240** ($100,000 principal plus $164,240 interest paid on the loan).

Example Two: 30-year loan at 8% interest with no extra principal payments but with payments made bi-weekly rather than once a month

593 payments (22 5/6 years times 26 payments per year) of $367 each for a total of **$217,844** ($100,000 principal plus $117,844 interest paid on the loan).

Example Three: 30-year loan at 8% interest with extra $100
              principal payment each month

240 payments (20 years times 12 payments per year) of $834 each (the extra $100 going to reduce the principal due) for a total of **$200,160** ($100,000 principal and $100,160 interest) paid on the loan.

Example Four: 15-year loan with no extra principal payments
              at 7½% interest (the interest rate is usually ½% lower with a 15-year loan)

180 payments (15 years times 12 payments per year) of $927 each for a total of **$166,860** ($100,000 principal plus $66,860 interest) paid on the loan.

Summary:

Example One: For 30 years at $734 per month with no extra principal payments, you'll pay $264,240 to age 60.

Example Two: For 22 5/6 years at $367 every two weeks, you'll pay $217,844 to age 53 and save almost $50,000 in interest payments as compared to Example One.

Example Three: For 20 years at $834 per month, you'll pay $200,160 to age 50 and save over $60,000 in interest payments as compared to Example One.

Example Four: For 15 years at $927 per month with no extra principal payments, you'll pay $166,860 to age 45 and save over $90,000 in interest payments as compared to Example One.

This summary illustrates how compound interest can work against you (i.e., 30-year loans) just as it can work for you in saving for retirement.

Some loans have penalties if you pay them off early (*prepayment penalties*). Even loans that have prepayment penalties usually allow you to pay off a certain amount each year without being subject to the penalty. Have your attorney check your loan documents on this matter.

Psychological considerations

In balancing the financial pros and cons, remember that a mortgage reduction plan offers the psychological advantage of making your mortgage go away faster and that can be worth a lot.

17.

Refinancing for the better

The biggest expense for most people is their home mortgage. One great way to cut down costs and provide extra funds may be to refinance the home mortgage when rates are advantageous.

Keep in mind, though, that if you take out a 30-year loan at age 40 and you do not pay additional principal over the years to reduce the lifespan of the loan (see pages 48-52), you could be making large mortgage payments until you're 70-years old.

Also, be aware that if you refinance, there may be a prepayment penalty (see page 52) and not all of the interest may be deductible (check with your accountant).

There is also one hidden aspect of refinancing that may affect your nest egg in an unexpected way.

When you buy a house and take out a loan as part of the purchase, some states give you special protection in that you may have no personal liability if you do not complete the payments on the mortgage. The lender in those cases may only go against the house and not your other assets to collect on the house loan.

When you refinance, you are probably giving up that protection because the refinanced loan was not taken out at the time of purchase. There may be circumstances where this personal liability potential could affect your decision to refinance.

This is one of several good reasons why your parents should probably avoid paying all cash for a retirement house (even if this luxury is possible) and then obtaining a loan later on. The same exposure to personal liability could apply to your parents even though they are not refinancing since this is the first time they're taking a loan out on the house.

Also, they'll be tying up a large portion of their assets in an illiquid (hard-to-sell) asset by paying all cash.

Finally, they may not be able to deduct all the interest on a loan taken out after the purchase of a property. Ask your accountant about limitations on deducting interest.

IMPROVING THE
QUALITY OF YOUR LIFE

18.

An apple a day

Take good care of yourself. You may think you're inde-
structible now but how will you be at age 95 if you live your
life that way? Health is more important than money for the
quality of your life. As an estate planning attorney, the one
regret I hear more often than anything else is a wish that a
person had been more conscious of health matters over the
years.

And part of taking care of your health is having health insurance. If you wait to apply for insurance once you're sick, you
won't be able to get insurance or your medical condition may
not be covered at all (or until after a lengthy waiting period
goes by).

19.

Adding value to your life

No matter how your financial bank accounts are doing, are you overdrawn or making regular deposits to your life values account?

Why wait until you retire to transform your life and/or work to make it more meaningful or spiritual?

Ask yourself whether you should be working and earning less but spending more time with your children and/or parents?

And, why wait until your life slows down to help society by volunteering? Check out http://www.servenet.org for a list of organizations in your area that are eager for volunteers.

Have you found your passion or purpose in life? Whether you have or not, sit down with pencil and paper and prepare your life values balance sheet of assets, liabilities, talents and desires. Try to give thanks each day for what has gone well and to learn from what hasn't.

20.

Simplifying your life

Simplification is becoming a major trend.

If you're facing a shortage of time and money (and who isn't?), one way to improve your lifestyle is to simplify it.

By reducing your material needs, you gain freedom to make career changes and life decisions without being shackled by a financial ball and chain.

Reducing paperwork and getting financial control

Here are some first steps in the right direction.

1. Consider automatic payouts for mortgage payments and health insurance premiums as well as automatic deductions from your paycheck or checking account for investments, retirement and college savings.

2. Have an automatic deposit of paychecks.

3. Limit and consolidate the number of investments, mutual funds and retirement plans to a manageable number so your assets are diversified, but not too many in number. Too many small investments can lead to chaos and cause you to give up on trying to monitor what's happening where.

4. Limit yourself to one credit card (two at most) and pay off the outstanding balance every month.

21.

Becoming a stay-at-home parent can pay off big

If you have children now or you're planning to in the future, you'll find this topic of interest.

Most families have two parents working outside the home. As a result, both parents are earning coverage under Social Security for retirement benefits. What is often overlooked is that those parents are also earning benefits for themselves and their family if they become disabled or pass away. These benefits can be significant (see pages 28, 29, 149 and 150).

Earning Social Security benefits

A stay-at-home parent who works part-time (a home business is permissible, too) can also earn Social Security benefits for himself or herself and the family. The Social Security *disability* or *survivors'* benefits can be critical in helping the family if a tragedy strikes the stay-at-home parent.

To qualify for these benefits, enough *quarters of coverage* need to be earned (there are different eligibility rules for the various types of benefits). A quarter of coverage is earned by having wages or self-employment income at a high enough level for a given year (the dollar amount can change every year). In 1997, for example, earnings (or profits after expenses of your own business) needed to be at least $670 to receive one quarter of coverage (you didn't have to earn $670 in a particular quarter—it's an annual test). So, earnings (or business profits) of $2,680 over the year 1997 would have earned four quarters of coverage.

A stay-at-home parent working part-time might provide an extra safety net of Social Security benefits to pull the family through a tough time.

The homeschooling option

Some stay-at-home parents are part of a growing trend— homeschooling. There are an estimated two million homeschoolers in the U.S. who come from all parts of society and are not just religious fundamentalists.

The ever-increasing presence of home offices provides the flexibility needed to combine parents working and children schooling at home.

Many parents are seriously considering this alternative for educational, spiritual and, in some cases, financial reasons. These are all concerned parents who recognize the importance of the family and the primary responsibility that parents have in transmitting their values directly to their children.

With kids spending six to eight hours a day at private or public school, plus commuting time and extracurricular activities, a parent's role has become secondary in many cases. By contrast, homeschooling offers the opportunity for parents to be a central part of a child's life.

Homeschooling parents, however, don't have to teach everything. Homeschooling children may have tutors and/or still go to school for certain classes and social activities but the home is the primary learning center (homeschoolers Ben Franklin and Abe Lincoln didn't turn out so badly).

Homeschooling at its best provides a quality education with real-life, hands-on experiences on a daily basis and a rich diversity of learning opportunities. Ideally, homeschooling isn't just taking the school model and bringing it home—it's really "lifeschooling," which utilizes every life opportunity as a learning opportunity. Homeschooling can allow parents to develop better relationships with their children.

What is the real benefit of a second income?

For those parents who feel they cannot give up part or all of a second income by homeschooling, they should another look at how little they really have left financially from a second income after federal and state income tax, Social Security and Medicare taxes, work-related expenses including commuting and child care expenses, and, in some cases, private school expenses.

Also, in some cases, the stay-at-home parent will receive the same amount of Social Security *retirement* benefits (by drawing on the other spouse's work record) as he or she would have received by working and paying into Social Security (*disability* and *survivors' benefits* are discussed on page 60).

Parents are reevaluating how much of their energy and lifeforce is used up at work each day rather than having these resources available for their children.

How much extra does a family net if both spouses rather than one spouse earns income? Take a look at this example of a possible scenario.

Assume one spouse earns $60,000 per year as an employee and the second spouse earns $30,000 per year in his or her own business. How much is really left of the second income?

Take a look at the example on the next page and then do your own life values calculations.

The real second income

Net income of second spouse's business after expenses but before taxes	$30,000
Less federal income tax on second income	(8,400)
Less state income tax on second income	(2,550)
Less employer's and employee's Social Security and Medicare tax if you have your own business	(4,590)
Less commuting and non-deductible (e.g., clothing, meals eaten away from home, etc.)	(2,000)
Less child care expenses	(3,500)
The Real Net Income	$ 8,960

And, if there is private school tuition in addition, the net amount left can evaporate completely.

In the future, home schooling may be on track to becoming as popular as home offices are now. Then, you'll tell your children about the old days, when you actually had to walk to school.

22.

Life insurance that pays while you're alive and ill

If you, a family member or a friend is "terminally ill" or "chronically ill" (as defined in the Internal Revenue Code), there may be a way to convert a life insurance policy into cash while the ill person is alive without being subject to federal (and maybe state) income tax. There are certain requirements, of course, and state laws need to reviewed, too. Your state department of insurance can provide useful information to help you make an informed decision.

There are two main types of lifetime payouts. If the insurance company pays you, it's sometimes called a "lifetime benefit," "living benefit" or "accelerated death benefit" (or "ADB"). See if your policy has an ADB rider or can have one added.

The payouts from the insurance company are usually higher than those from third-party companies. If a third-party company pays you, it's called a "viatical settlement."

These payouts can preserve a dignity of life for the terminally ill person by providing needed funds at a critical time.

In some cases, it can even be used for estate planning purposes by providing funds to make death-bed gifts to reduce the size of one's estate for death tax purposes.

However, it is not always beneficial to cash in a life insurance policy while one is alive. Life insurance proceeds paid instead after a death might be free of creditor's claims.

23.

Protecting your privacy

There is too much information out there about everyone. Personal information accumulates and grows. It's like a bacteria that can't be killed, only controlled.

It's your responsibility to minimize the exposure of your financial and personal information to keep undesirables from using your financial resources and/or identity to their advantage.

Just say no!

Many times it's unnecessary for you to give out your birthdate, driver's license number, Social Security number, credit card number or your mother's maiden name. If you can't see the absolute necessity for providing *any* of the above pieces of information (try never to give anyone all of the above except a credit reporting agency such as Trans Union), then leave that space blank on a form and ask whether it's absolutely necessary to provide the private information.

For more information on protecting yourself, you may also want to contact the Privacy Rights Clearinghouse. The Clearinghouse offers consumers information on how to protect their personal privacy (http://www.privacyrights.org or 1/619/298-3396, California). You should consider purchasing *The Privacy Rights Handbook* (see page 154 for more information).

Credit reports

There are three large credit reporting agencies listed below. You can get a free report from them if you live in certain states or if you've been denied credit (or under certain other circumstances). If you don't qualify for a free report, ask the agencies about obtaining a joint report at a reduced cost.

If you're about to buy a house, it's wise to check your credit report and correct any errors before applying for a home loan. Also, if your children are going to apply for loans to pay for college based on your credit, you'll want to clear up any errors which might prevent them from qualifying for school loans. Periodically, it's not a bad idea to see what's shown in all three of your credit reports.

The big three credit reporting agencies are:

Equifax
> 1/800/685-1111 to request a copy of your credit report
> 1/800/556-4711 to have your name removed from mailings

Experian
> 1/800/682-7654 to request a copy of your credit report
> 1/800/353-0809 to have your name removed from mailings

Trans Union
> 1/800/851-2674 to request a copy of your credit report
> 1/800/680-7293 to have your name removed from mailings

Keeping an eye on who's keeping an eye on you

You'll want to see who's looking at your credit files and also receive regular updates of your files from the three credit reporting agencies. American Express has started to offer the CreditAware service (1/800/964-3596) to help consumers be sure their credit reports from the three agencies read the same and are accurate.

MOVING TO GREENER PASTURES

24.

Five questions you need to ask before moving to a new state or staying right where you are

Most of us assume we can live anywhere in the United States and the laws and rules will be pretty much the same. That isn't the case.

There are five questions you need to ask before making a move. Your parents need to get the answers to these questions, too, before they start packing their bags.

1. Are the income tax laws different in the new state and will I still be subject to income tax in the old state after I move?

There are different state income tax laws across the country. As your parents look for a place to retire, you might remind them to consider seek out a state without an income tax. If they earned a pension in a state with an income tax and then moved to a state with no income tax, there's a good chance that the old state cannot tax the pension. They need to ask their accountant whether income tax authorities of the first state can follow the pension income to the new state to tax it. Congress has passed limitations on the old states taxing pensions in most cases.

2. Will my will or trust work the same in the new state?

The laws for wills, trusts and inheritance are not identical in every state. Everyone who moves to a new state should have

THE GENERATION X MONEY BOOK

his or her will or trust reviewed by an attorney in the new state to be sure no surprises arise down the line. For example, in these days of blended families, it's important to ask an attorney in the new state what the rights, if any, would be for step-children if you did not revise your will or trust.

3. Will my marital agreement be enforceable in the new state?

A marital agreement valid in one state may not be enforceable if you move to another state. Also, the rules for the necessary elements in the agreement may be different, depending upon whether the agreement was signed before or after the marriage. You might need to sign another agreement in the new state if your spouse is agreeable.

Some states use a community property concept of ownership while most use a separate property approach. Find out whether you'll be affected by a move to a new state.

4. Are the inheritance tax laws the same in both states?

Talk to your legal and financial advisor about whether the inheritance tax laws are more favorable in one state as compared to another and whether you should take certain steps (e.g., voting in the new state, getting a driver's license in the new state, signing a will or trust in the new state, etc.) to establish a *domicile* (i.e., permanent residence) to determine where you should be taxed. Also, find out if you can avoid having a probate upon your death in any state, let alone in more than one state.

If you split your time between two or more states, both states may try to take a tax bite out of your estate at your death. Or, one state may have no inheritance tax and the other state may have a steep tax and you can guess which one would like to go after a piece of your estate.

5. Are the health insurance laws the same in new state?

Some states offer more liberal or more restrictive health insurance coverage. Check it out before a move is made.

25.

Finding the right place for your parents to retire

There's a good chance you'll need to help take care of your parents.

Physical proximity to your parents can be of great comfort to them and to you. It can also help you avoid disruptions at work, which is important in these days of job insecurity.

When our parents need us, there's usually a crisis that may linger on for years. With blended families, we may be stretched out literally and figuratively as parents, step-parents, siblings, and step-siblings relocate across the country.

There are financial implications relating to where one lives. For example, different states have different rules for determining eligibility for governmental assistance in paying for nursing home costs. Don't assume that because you have become educated about the rules in one state (and that your parents would qualify in that state) that your parents will qualify if they move to another state. This is an important item to be checked out with an attorney before any final decisions are made by your parents.

These possibilities point up the good sense of obtaining legal advice on how to sever ties with a state (e.g., voting in the new state, getting a driver's license in the new state, signing a will or trust in the new state, signing a declaration of domicile, etc.) and whether it is advisable to do so.

LOOKING OUT
FOR YOUR PARENTS

26.

Telling your parents the financial facts of life before they remarry

On pages 87 through 94, you'll read about the many issues you face when you marry or remarry. These same issues apply to your parents, too, and there may even be another issue.

When our parents marry a new spouse, they very often want their assets to go to their children and original family.

Assuming the new couple (1) signs a marital agreement saying what's mine is mine and what's yours is yours, (2) signs new wills and/or trusts, (3) coordinates how title (ownership) on assets is set up so that it works with and not against the wills and trusts, and (4) signs any needed waivers on retirement plan benefits to allow children to benefit, there is still another issue for your parents to consider.

What will happen to the assets of *both* spouses if shortly after the remarriage, the senior citizen bride or groom needs long-term nursing home care? The expectation of the couple might be that the assets of the well spouse cannot be touched. Most people would imagine that once the assets of the ill spouse were exhausted, then governmental aid for nursing home costs could be obtained.

However, the law in your parent's state may delay governmental assistance until some or most of the assets of the well spouse are used to pay for nursing home costs (or the government might be able to make a claim against the assets of the well spouse after the death of the well spouse). This can apply even if a marital agreement has been signed saying each parent pay his or her own way. Legal advice should be obtained to see how the law works in your parent's state.

This scenario may mean that this short remarriage results in depriving one of the ability to pass on an inheritance from a lifetime of work to one's children. Even worse, this is a case where saying "I do" can really mean "I'm elderly and could soon be broke." Long-term care (i.e., nursing home insurance) can help prevent this result.

Before your parent ties the knot, they should check to see whether Social Security benefits will be affected by the marriage. For example, a divorced person claiming benefits on an ex-spouse's working record could lose those benefits by remarrying.

27.

The joint tenancy surprise: the down side of holding title as joint tenants

Joint tenancy means more than just a way to avoid probate in the event of a death. It can also have negative effects when parents and children hold ownership of assets together as joint tenants.

Financial risk of joint tenancy

If your parents put you and/or your brothers and sisters (or anyone else) on title as joint tenants on any of their assets, all of the joint tenants are co-owners of the jointly-owned assets (e.g., a house) while your parents are alive.

Besides gift tax, income tax, property tax, and death tax issues arising from joint tenancy, parents are taking a financial risk when they hold title as joint tenants with their children.

Although joint tenancy may afford more protection from creditors after the death of one of the joint tenants, it can lead to more exposure to creditors while all the joint tenants are alive.

If, for example, one of your brothers or sisters has a business that goes under, then the creditors of that sibling may go after the sibling's portion of your parents' house while your parents are alive. If one of your siblings is at fault in a car accident where their car insurance is not enough to cover the damage, the injured party may also go after your sibling's portion of your parents' house while your parents are alive. In either of these examples the creditor could become a co-owner with your parents or possibly force a sale of the house (maybe even charge your parents rent for the interest in the house owned by the creditor).

So, if your parents want to avoid probate and also avoid being responsible for their children's debts and actions, they should talk to their attorney about setting up a *living trust* instead. A living trust is an arrangement that spells out who is to be the manager and beneficiary of assets while your parents are alive and after each of them passes away. A living trust, which is in essence a substitute for a will, allows successors to avoid the probate court after a death. (To be fully effective, however, certain asset transfers to the trust need to be done before a death.)

The bottom line is that while a technique such as joint tenancy may be good for one purpose (e.g., avoiding probate), it can have other, unintended, disastrous effects.

Also, if parents and children hold title as joint tenants and pass away simultaneously, such as in a car accident or a plane crash, the jointly held assets (e.g., a house, bank accounts, stocks, etc.) may go through several probates: the parents' and the children's. So, in such cases joint tenancy may not even give the benefit of avoiding probate.

Joint tenancy may disinherit intended beneficiaries

What do you think happens in this scenario: Your parents sign wills leaving everything equally to all of their four children, including you. They put one of your siblings on title to everything they own as a joint tenant. Both of your parents pass away. Who gets your parents' assets?

In general, it's going to be one person, the one sibling who was on title as a joint tenant.

A will or trust generally does not control assets held in joint tenancy. Unless an exception applies, assets held in joint tenancy pass outside of a will or trust to the surviving joint tenant.

In the above example, your parents probably wanted the one child to be able sign checks or take actions on their behalf if they became disabled. They probably did not want to give all of their assets to the one child.

Again, a living trust might be a safer way of dealing with disability or incompetency.

The bottom line is that you and your siblings should not have to face the joint tenancy surprise. Encourage your parents to see an attorney who can explain their options to them.

28.

The income tax surprise
all siblings need to know

If your parents leave you and your sibling equal shares of their estate, you can accidentally wind up with less than your sibling. Your share may be the one that's subject to income tax.

Assume that your parents have two main assets (their house and their IRAs) and they are thinking of leaving them to their two children—you and your sibling.

If the house is worth about the same as the IRAs and you and your sibling don't get along well, your parents might think they were doing you a favor (and not harming either of you in any way) by leaving the house to your sibling and the IRAs to you. After all, this would avoid co-ownership and possibly fights between your sibling and you.

Your parents unfortunately made this decision before obtaining legal and tax advice so they weren't aware of the different consequences to you and your sibling. If your sibling inherits the house, it may never be subject to income tax. If you receive the IRAs, it *may* be income (depending upon the type of IRA and the holding period) to you and you may be paying income tax on all or a portion of the amount received. The solution is for your parents to get legal and tax advice so their estates are planned properly.

29.

The death tax surprise
all siblings need to know

Depending on how your parents' wills, trusts and beneficiary designations read, you may have the pleasure of paying death tax on assets inherited by your sibling.

Very often, wills and trusts stipulate that all the death taxes be paid from the "residue" of the estate covered by the documents.

Certain assets may pass automatically outside a will or trust upon a death such as joint tenancy assets and assets that have beneficiary designations (e.g., IRAs and life insurance).

Assume that your parents have two main assets (their house and their IRAs) and death tax will be due. In their wills they leave the house to you and they leave the IRAs under beneficiary designations to your sibling.

The wills might say death taxes on everything (including assets passing outside the will such as IRAs) will be paid from the assets (the house) covered by the will. This means that you would pay the death taxes on the house you inherited and on the IRAs *inherited by your sibling*. Is this what your parents intended? Again, make sure your parents get legal advice to properly plan their estates to avoid this tax result.

30.

Mentioning the unmentionable

We all have a reluctance to discuss terminal illness and death. Your parents should discuss both of these issues with the family and put their desires in writing. You should do the same to help your loved ones.

Terminal illness

There are two basic legal documents for handling a terminal illness: (1) a *health power of attorney* and (2) a *living will* (also sometimes called a *directive to physician* or *natural death declaration*).

A health power of attorney appoints an agent to make all the big and small health care decisions if one isn't able to speak for himself or herself. The biggest decision is whether to "pull the plug" (i.e., to be taken off life-support machines).

Your parents need to completely trust the agent they are naming. They should consider whether that person has any financial conflict of interest. For example, will the agent inherit from your parents if the plug is pulled? Often that's the case but that fact alone shouldn't rule a person out. Also, the agent should not have personal or religious beliefs that would prevent fulfillment of your parents' desired wishes.

The *living will* deals just with the big issue, pulling the plug. It's usually put into effect if there's an incurable and irreversible condition that has been diagnosed by two physicians and the condition either (1) will result in death within a relatively short time without the administration of life-sustaining treatment, or (2) has produced an irreversible coma or persistent vegetative state in which one is no longer able to make decisions regarding his or her medical treatment.

Under such circumstances, a living will directs the attending physician to withhold or withdraw treatment that only prolongs an irreversible coma, a persistent vegetative state, or the process of dying. Such treatment is defined as "not necessary for your comfort or to alleviate pain" and could include the use of a respirator as well as artificially administered nutrition and hydration.

Spelling out funeral arrangements

If a will spells out funeral arrangements and is placed in a safe deposit box, it's possible no one may have access to the box until after the funeral is over.

Loved ones (and one's executor) should know in advance what is desired and also whether any arrangements have been made such as prepaid funeral or cremation costs.

Expressing desires in writing can avoid confusion or misunderstandings at a time when everyone is grieving.

A direction for funeral arrangements should cover at least the following items:

1. Donation of body organs
2. Nature of the desired ceremony (if any)—indicate whether it's to be religious or non-religious, elaborate or private
3. Name, address, phone number and title of the person to officiate
4. Any special readings, passages or prayers to be included as part of the service
5. Name and location of cemetery

6. Directions regarding burial (headstone/monument requests) or cremation (disposition of ashes)
7. Any prepayments that have been made.

TYING OR RETYING
THE KNOT

31.

What you must know before you marry or remarry

Whether you are planning to marry for the first time or get remarried, you need to do some advance planning to avoid some surprises down the road.

You'll want to consider how title (ownership) is taken on assets each of you owns now and may own in the future, such as bank accounts and a house, so that the intended beneficiaries inherit upon a death.

For example, if you own assets with your spouse as joint tenants, your children from a former marriage may get nothing upon your death even if your will leaves everything to them. Why? Because, in general, certain ways of holding title (ownership) such as joint tenancy *override* a will or trust.

How you take title may also impact how assets will be divided in case this marriage (or remarriage) doesn't work out.

Title to assets can also affect income taxes for the surviving spouse and death taxes for the family.

You should sign a new will and/or trust after getting married. If you don't do so, the law will probably assume that you wanted to carve out a sizeable share or all of your estate for your spouse but just never got around to doing so.

You need to think through the provisions of a new will or trust. You might say, "I want to leave everything to my kids from my former marriage." What if your spouse sold his or her residence to move into your house? You may want to provide for your surviving spouse. Would you want your spouse to have to move out right after your death or would you instead allow your spouse some time to live there and plan the next move? Would your spouse be paying rent or taking care of expenses on the residence during that time period? What about the furnishings in the residence? If they had belonged to you, would you want your spouse left without a stick of furniture? Take a look pages 93 and 94 for additional suggestions in providing for a surviving spouse and protecting your children from a former marriage.

If you have young children, you'll need to think about who should be named as the guardian to raise them.

Coordinate your will and/or trust with the beneficiary designations on your IRAs, retirement plans and life insurance to take advantage of all available income tax and death tax benefits. You should update your will and trust for tax changes, too, such as the 1997 tax act. And, if you or your spouse are not U.S. citizens, make sure your estate plan has all needed special provisions to prevent death tax surprises.

See page 90 to see how your marriage could affect college financial aid.

All of these issues and others such as retirement plan and IRA payouts need to be coordinated in a master plan worked out with your attorney so that no element is working at cross purposes with the rest of the plan. You should review with your attorney, before the marriage, your potential liability for debts of your spouse, including tax obligations.

Before you go to the altar, go to your attorney to discuss the reasons for considering a marital agreement.

Finally, take a look at pages 75 and 84, which discusses considerations for your parents' remarrying because these issues may apply to you, too.

32.

Will Uncle Sam tear up part of your marital agreement?

Assume you signed a beneficiary designation naming your two children from a prior marriage as the beneficiaries on your retirement plan. Then you remarry and a marital agreement is signed saying what's yours is yours and what's mine is mine, including retirement plan assets. After the remarriage, you sign a new will and a beneficiary designation leaving everything to your children. If this new marriage lasts two years and then you pass away, who will get the retirement assets?

It may be that your surviving spouse will receive all of the benefits through an annuity that lasts for the spouse's lifetime. Why? Depending upon the type of retirement plan, federal law may say that your spouse must be the sole beneficiary because your spouse never signed a necessary *waiver* form after the marriage concerning retirement plan benefits.

This can distort your intended result, especially if the retirement plan is a major asset in the estate. Talk to your attorney about the steps you can take to avoid this confusion.

33.

Filling out college aid applications before and after the wedding

Becoming a step-parent can have quite an impact on a child's or step-child's chance of qualifying for college aid programs.

If you're a single parent, you are not reporting the income and assets of anyone except yourself.

Once you get married (or remarried), you are then part of a team and the financial situation of the entire team needs to be considered.

Federal aid programs consider the income of the custodial parents. If you are not yet married, then your children are not reporting the income of your spouse-to-be. When you and your spouse say "I do," each of you may be saying "I'll pay" for the college education of your step-children when they have a second custodial parent.

That means the financial picture of both parents enters into the equation to determine *eligibility* for college aid, even if you've signed a pre-marital agreement saying each of you will pay for your own children's education. Ask your attorney whether your state law requires a different arrangement.

34.

For better or for worse—what can that *really* mean?

Before you tie the knot, you should get advice on your potential liability as a spouse and on ways to protect your assets.

You need to know the implications of putting your new spouse on title to the residence you brought into the marriage. Will the house be sold if your spouse's business venture goes belly up? Will the house be sold due to a debt incurred before the marriage that was never paid off? How will the house be divided if the marriage breaks up?

Divorce settlements as to the division of the home may change due to the change in the federal tax law (see page 45).

Buy some time for a consultation with an attorney so you can ease your concerns and enjoy your marriage.

Before you *un*tie the knot and get a divorce, ask whether you'll qualify for Social Security benefits under your soon-to-be ex-spouse's working record by staying in the marriage for a bit longer.

Do you want your ex-spouse to inherit from you?

Consider the following scenario: You pass away and leave everything directly to your two young children. What happens if one of them then passes away without having a will or trust and without having a surviving spouse or child of their own? State law may say that your child's closest relative, your ex-spouse, will inherit the child's assets (including what your child inherited from you).

Instead of leaving assets outright and in the pockets of your children, you might want to put some strings on the assets such as creating trusts for your children.

Talk to your attorney about how such trusts could be written. Keep in mind that it will cost more now in attorney's fees to have trust provisions written as compared to leaving your assets outright to your children. Also, there will be greater legal and accounting costs through the years after your death in connection with such trusts for your children.

If your worst nightmare is the possibility of your ex-spouse inheriting your hard-earned assets, please discuss this matter with your attorney. After you obtain the needed information, you'll be able to make the right decision (and sleep at night).

35.

Protecting the inheritance for your kids

If you are in your first marriage or a remarriage, there is a way you can benefit your spouse under your will or trust but also make sure your children are the beneficiaries of what's left over after your spouse passes away.

To get this result, you need to have a will or trust that leaves assets in trust (rather than outright) to your surviving spouse. This type of trust gives you some control over assets left to benefit your spouse (also see pages 133 and 134). It allows your spouse to benefit from your assets but at the same time gives you the final say as to the ultimate beneficiaries once your surviving spouse passes away (even if your spouse remarries).

The best planning in a will or trust will all go out the window unless you hold title (ownership) to your assets in a way that complements your intended plan. Otherwise, assets may pass outside the will or trust to unintended beneficiaries.

You'll also need to review with your attorney how beneficiary designations on life insurance, IRA, 401(k), and other retirement plans should read after a marriage. You may need to have your spouse sign a special waiver so certain retirement benefits go to someone other than your spouse (e.g., your children from a prior marriage).

If you are remarrying and you and/or your future spouse have children from a former marriage, talk to your attorney about how your will or trust may benefit or exclude step-children. If you don't deal with this issue, it may be that upon your death your state law will give step-children and your children equal shares of your estate. This is fine if it's what you want to happen. But do your family a favor and don't have everyone guessing and paying attorney's fees to sort things out after your death.

Some wills and trusts tie the size of the children's inheritance from a first marriage to the amount of the federal estate tax exemption ($600,000 in 1997). The exemption increased in 1998 (to $625,000) and it will increase each year until the year 2006 (when it will be $1,000,000). If your pre-1997 tax act will or trust says give the maximum exempt amount to the children, would your children receive $600,000, $1,000,000 or something in-between? Have your estate plan reviewed to avoid confusion.

Finally, be sure that your will and/or trust says who will pay death taxes. Otherwise, it could be that your spouse or a child receives an asset outside the will or trust but only the beneficiaries under the will or trust pay the death taxes on that asset. This could result in a total depletion of assets passing under the will or trust.

KIDS, STEP-KIDS
AND COLLEGE

36.

The right and wrong ways to save for your children's college education (and maybe pay for your own)

It's a special challenge to try to save for personal security and independence, retirement and at the same time save for a child's (or your own) college education.

A child born in 1998 will need around $116,000 to cover all the expenses for four years at a public university. This translates to saving $227 per month from the time the child is born. A more realistic goal per child is to try to save up to one-half of the public university cost—$113 per month. The cost for a child attending a private university is double the amount for a public university. The numbers become astronomical for a family with two or three children.

What's a person to do? How can limited resources be split between personal financial planning and funding a child's college education?

Before investing one penny for a child's college education, the first step is to determine whether investments should be made in the parents' names or the child's. The consequences of this decision on a child qualifying for college financial aid down the line are enormous. This decision not only affects a child's ability to qualify for college education financial aid, it can also have income tax, death tax and other implications.

There are five basic sources for paying for a child's college education: (1) scholarships, (2) the child's earnings while going to school, (3) the child's savings, including any Education IRAs, (4) the parents' savings, and (5) financial aid. In most cases, it will take a combination of two or more of these sources to fund a college education.

The fifth source, financial aid, is very dependent upon the amount of a child's savings and, to a much lesser degree, the parents' savings, assets and income. Prior to opening up savings accounts and purchasing stocks, bonds and life insurance policies to fund a college education, you need to look at the long-term consequences of these actions.

Save in your name?

The key decision is whether you should save college money in your name or your child's. You should make this decision as early as possible since it affects qualifying for college education financial aid and has tax implications, too.

Currently, colleges require students to spend much more of their money (over 33%) as compared to their parents' money (less than 10%) to pay for college education. This makes sense since students should pay to the extent they are capable of doing so. This approach will also make many parents set up a college savings fund in their names rather than their children's.

Another incentive to invest in your name is the income tax benefits with certain U.S. Savings Bonds. If these bonds are purchased in your name, used to pay for your children's college education and your income does not exceed certain limits, you can exclude the bond interest from your income for federal income tax purposes. Since this exclusion phases out as your income gets higher, you need to estimate your future income before deciding upon the actual benefit of this approach. You may want to carefully time when you cash in these bonds to maximize eligibility for aid.

To find out what a U.S. Savings Bond is worth at any given time, http://www.publicdebt.treas.gov/sav/savrepor.htm is the Internet address for the government's Internet Web site. You can also write the Bureau of Public Debt, Savings Bond Operation Office, Parkersburg WV 26106-1328 and request PD-3600 ("Table of Redemption Values").

Blended families

One danger of investing in your name, especially with blended families (i.e., children from a prior marriage on one or both sides), is what can happen to the money if the blended family breaks up and a divorce occurs or if you pass away. Will half or more of the "college education fund" in your name that was intended for the education of your children from a former marriage instead be divided up with your current spouse? Get legal advice now so the correct result occurs.

Save in your child's name?

When parents put money or other assets in the names of their minor children to pay for future college expenses, they usually do it under the *Uniform Transfers to Minors Act* ("UTMA") or the *Uniform Gifts to Minors Act* ("UGMA").

In general, with UTMA or UGMA, you can retain control as the manager (called the custodian) until the designated age (age 18 or sometimes age 21) is attained by a child of yours. If you do not take certain steps when you set up the investments and you pass away before a child reaches the designated age, these assets that were "owned" by your child may be taxed in your estate for death tax purposes. You should consult with your attorney on how to avoid that result.

Another risk of using UTMA or UGMA is that once a child reaches the designated age, the child is entitled to receive all of the assets in the account and use them in any manner. Your children may not want to use the funds to go to or stay in college.

The 1997 tax act and getting professional advice

The 1997 tax act has created a dizzying array of options and possibilities. Some of the new benefits have side effects that may lead to a corresponding reduction of another education aid benefit (leaving you no better off). The complexity in this area will probably cause you to seek professional advice. Try to find a tax advisor who is already knowledgeable about all of the options discussed in this section and is not becoming introduced to these topics and educated at your expense.

Education IRAs

The 1997 tax act created Education IRAs that allow contributions of up to $500 per child per calendar year from a child's birth through his or her 18th birthday. So, that's a maximum of 18 times $500 or $9,000 in contributions (by age 18, there might be over $40,000 in this IRA between contributions and growth). Here you're saving in your child's name.

The contributions are *not* tax deductible but the earnings grow income tax free and the withdrawals are not subject to federal income tax or penalties when used for certain college related purposes. If the money is used for another purpose, it is subject to income tax plus a tax penalty.

Not everyone qualifies to set up these Education IRAs. There are limits on the amount of your income (the limits may change from year to year) and state laws may need to be conformed for this tax benefit, too. If your income is too high to establish an Education IRA, maybe your parents qualify to make the contribution. Grandparents are eligible contributors, too.

There are some restrictions. In the same year, money cannot be put away in both an Education IRA and a prepaid tuition plan for the same child.

Also, financial aid will probably be reduced for those persons with Education IRAs. This may also happen where there are traditional IRAs and/or Roth IRAs—be on the lookout for developments in this area.

And, once your child is in college, the Education IRA cannot have a tax-free withdrawal in the same year you want to benefit from the Hope (tax) Credit described below.

Hope (tax) Credits for education

The 1997 tax act also allows certain taxpayers to take tax credits on their federal income tax return (subject to income limits, too) for certain college expenses. Credits, unlike deductions, can reduce income tax dollar for dollar. Credits are better than deductions. In other words, a $1,500 tax *credit* may reduce your income tax by $1,500. A $1,500 tax *deduction* reduces your income tax by $1,500 times your tax bracket (i.e., if you're in the 28% tax bracket, that's 28% times $1,500 for a $420 income tax reduction).

There are limits on the level of your income for you to qualify for this tax benefit (the limits may change from year to year) and state laws will need to conform to allow for this tax benefit, too. This program gives parents an incentive to delay income, if possible, during the first two years a child is in college. Also, the credit may be reduced by scholarships, grants and other benefits.

The credit can be up to $1,500 per year for the first two years of college (that's a dollar-for-dollar tax credit for the first $1,000 of qualified expenses and then one-half of the next $1,000 of qualified expenses for the first two years of college). Starting with the third year of college, there can be an annual credit of up $1,000 (20% of qualified expenses). After the year 2002, the 20% credit can be $2,000 per year up to a lifetime amount of $10,000 for additional years in college.

Since you can't have the Education IRA and the credit in the same year, you'll need to decide between the two benefits. Check with your accountant as to whether the tax credit or the Education IRA will be more beneficial for you.

Other IRAs as sources

Another provision of the 1997 tax act is that traditional IRAs can be used penalty free (but not income-tax free) for educational expenses of children and grandchildren. Of course, then that money would not be available for retirement purposes and the IRA withdrawals would increase your income for financial aid purposes. From time-to-time, double-check the current rules as to whether these IRAs harm your child's eligibility for college financial aid.

Roth IRAs may be used penalty free for educational expenses and also possibly income-tax free (if all requirements are met). If you have a Roth IRA, ask your tax advisor whether you can avoid income tax and penalties by just withdrawing your Roth IRA contributions, but not the growth.

This area is so technical that you should check with your tax advisor before withdrawing money from any source for educational purposes.

Other possible sources

There are a variety of other sources that may be appropriate for you in accumulating college education dollars.

Tuition prepayment plans. One possibility is to sign up for a tuition prepayment plan that guarantees the payments you make will cover tuition expenses regardless of future increases. What these plans do *not* guarantee is admission for your children to the institution of higher learning or, in most cases, whether the state will guarantee the safety of your money if the tuition plan has financial problems. Since you will be paying a fee through a reduced return to obtain this future cost protection, you need to compare the rate of return on this investment (and the institution's rules on withdrawals if you change your mind or your child does not want to go to college) with other forms of investing. Check with your accountant each year to see if the rules allow you to put away money in both an Education IRA and a tuition prepayment plan in the same year.

Life insurance policies. What about a life insurance policy on you that has a cash value building up inside it as a way to save for college? Since term life policies do not have a cash value build-up, you could consider using a non-term life insurance policy (probably a *variable cash value life insurance policy*) that invests in a mutual fund with growth stocks.

Consider the risks, however, because if the investments do not work out, you can lose not only your cash value in the policy *but also* your coverage as well. On the other hand, if the investments do work out, you can reduce the size of your premium payments. The value inside such a policy would increase free of any income taxes. At college entrance time you could tap that cash value.

Instead of cashing in the policy to pay for college expenses, you could withdraw the cash value in a non-taxable policy loan to pay for college expenses. If you should die before your children were ready for college, the amount available would be even larger due to the life insurance component of the policy. And, yes, these death benefits could pass income-tax free to your children.

Usually it makes sense to use life insurance only if you need the insurance anyway and there are ten or more years until your children are applying for college since the surrender charges and fees may be too high compared with the return.

Alternative service and other schools

Consider utilizing community/junior colleges and vocational schools as alternative or complementary education sources.

Don't overlook the educational benefits offered in return for service given to our country including military service, AmeriCorps and other national programs.

Student loans. Another source is student loans where some interest may be tax-deductible. Find out how much of the interest can be tax-deductible and for what period of time. These student loans are probably a better source than totally non-deductible credit card loans.

Finding financial aid

Call 1/800/433-3243 for the U.S. Department of Education's guide *Funding Your Education.*

For a wealth of information, take a look at the Web site of the National Association of Student Financial Aid Administrators (http://www.finaid.org).

Home equity loans. As last resorts to be avoided if possible, you might tap into the equity in your home or a retirement plan to raise necessary funds. Ask your accountant about the limits on deducting interest on home equity loans and the possible income tax consequences of early withdrawals from a retirement plan.

Steps to consider while a child is in high school

Usually two or three years in advance of college entrance time, you'll look into changing the form of any higher-risk tuition investment (e.g., certain stocks and mutual funds) into a safer one producing a fixed rate of return (e.g., certificates of deposit).

One way to plan for the conversion of funds automatically is to purchase *zero-coupon municipal bonds*. With these bonds, you pay a discounted price now (e.g., $600) and when the bond matures, you receive the full price ($1,000). Your purchase of zero-coupon bonds can be staggered to mature one-fourth each year for four years. Of course, these days students are not usually graduating in just four years. You might want to build in a fifth year plan, too.

Another approach is to encourage your children to take advanced placement classes and tests to obtain college credit while in high school. This is one way to shorten the college tuition duration. Maybe you could offer your children a financial bonus if they get college credits in high school (e.g., give your children one-half of the savings for the earned units).

As tuition time rolls around, grandparents may want to help out. Although there is a federal gift tax exclusion for gifts of up to $10,000 per recipient per calendar year (the $10,000 will be adjusted for inflation), there are two ways to increase that amount. A grandparent can take care of a grandchild's unreimbursable, qualified medical expenses by making a payment directly to the health care provider (medical insurance comes under this, too) and a grandparent can handle a grandchild's educational expenses making a payment directly to the educational institution. And, a Roth IRA may qualify to be used income-tax free to pay tuition of a grandchild. All in all, grandparents may want to reduce potential death taxes by paying their grandchild's tuition by some of these gift approaches.

If all else fails

All of the these tax benefits for education costs have different eligibility requirements tied to the level of your income. If you still fall short of funds even after utilizing all available benefits and programs, remember that you may be able to negotiate with colleges in paying tuition costs.

37.

Calculating a college-size nest egg

The nest egg for a private university will probably need to be twice as large as one for a public university.

For a student entering college in 1998, the four-year total cost (tuition, books, room and board and other expenses) is around $48,000 for a public university and around $96,000 for a private university. As each year goes by, inflation will probably increase these costs at a 5% per year rate. That means an eight-year old will face public university costs of nearly $80,000 and private university costs close to $160,000.

These staggering costs point up the need to start saving now, even if it means using a piggy bank. The good news is that you can cut in half the amount you need to save if your children go to a public university.

Should you plan to save all of the costs?

It may be unrealistic for you to assume you can save 100% of these probable college costs. Whatever you can save will be a big help. If you can manage to save one-half or two-thirds of the needed amount, you will have achieved a great deal. Any savings you already have in place for college costs will also reduce the monthly amount needed to accumulate the desired college nest egg. Your children may be able to pay for the difference through loans, scholarships or other financial aid, including work-study programs.

The effect of inflation on college costs

The table below assumes your child enters college at age 18
and shows how 5% per year inflation will drive up private
and public college education costs.

Your child's year of birth	Total 4-year cost at private university	Total 4-year cost at public university
1984	$117,209	$58,604
1985	123,069	61,535
1986	129,223	64,611
1987	135,684	67,842
1988	142,468	71,234
1989	149,591	74,796
1990	157,072	78,536
1991	164,925	82,463
1992	173,171	86,586
1993	181,830	90,915
1994	190,922	95,461
1995	200,468	100,233
1996	210,489	105,245
1997	221,014	110,507
1998	232,064	116,032
1999	243,668	121,834
2000	255,851	127,925
2001	268,644	134,322
2002	282,076	141,038
2003	296,180	148,090

The next table shows how much you will need to save each
month to reach your goal.

Your child's year of birth	Monthly savings for 50% of public university cost	Monthly savings for 50% of private university cost or 100% of public university cost
1984	$488	$977
1985	393	786
1986	330	659
1987	284	568
1988	250	500
1989	223	446
1990	202	403
1991	184	368
1992	169	338
1993	156	313
1994	145	291
1995	136	272
1996	128	255
1997	120	240
1998	113	227
1999	119	238
2000	125	250
2001	131	263
2002	138	276
2003	145	290

The first monthly savings column shows the amount of monthly savings you'd need to reach 50% of the expected public university cost. The second monthly savings column shows both the amount of monthly savings for 50% of the private university cost or 100% of the public university cost—they are the same amount since it costs about twice as much for a private university.

The last table was based on starting to save for college costs from scratch on January 1, 1999, earning 8% per year (before taxes) on the investments and reinvesting all the earnings. However, if your child is born in 2000 or later, then the table assumes you started to save on January 1 of the year in which your child was born.

The earlier you start, the smaller your monthly nut

The last table shows is the benefit of starting to save early. If your goal is to save 50% of the cost of a four-year education in a public university for a child born in 1999, you can achieve that goal under the stated assumptions by saving $119 per month when the child is born. If you delay saving for that same child until the child is three years away from entering college, to reach the 50% public education cost goal you'd need to save around $1,500 *per month* (that calculation is not in the table).

To meet your savings goal, you should try to set up an arrangement whereby funds are withdrawn automatically from your checking account and put into your college fund investments. Each year, you should review with your financial advisor both the rate of return on your investments and the college cost inflation rate to see that you are staying on schedule in your savings program.

INSURING YOUR FUTURE

38.

The three questions you should ask about life insurance—before you buy

Before you buy life insurance, always ask yourself *and* your life insurance agent these three questions:

1. Why do I need this insurance?

2. What is the most this policy will cost me and for how many years under a worst-case scenario?

3. How much will I lose if I decide to cancel the policy early?

Do you need life insurance?

The first step in deciding whether to purchase life insurance is to determine your needs, which could include any of the following:

1. Making life more comfortable for a surviving spouse and/or children

2. Having enough money to raise and educate children in case of a death

3. Having a ready source of cash to pay death taxes so assets such as real estate or a family business won't have to be liquidated to meet tax obligations

4. Providing the funds to buy out the interest of a business partner if the partner dies

5. Paying for funeral costs and legal expenses upon a death

6. Building up a source of retirement income and assets.

If you have more than one need, then you may want more than one policy and/or more than one type of policy (for types of policies, see pages 120 and 121).

Not everyone, however, needs life insurance. For example, single persons with no dependents (i.e., no children or parents or other individuals dependent on them) may not need any life insurance other than to cover funeral costs.

Worst-case scenario

Before you purchase life insurance, you are usually handed a lengthy computer printout. On the printout are many columns with calculations explaining the cost and benefits of a policy.

This printout includes an optimistic projection (estimate) of your future costs and benefits. You also need to see in writing what the guaranteed result would be. In other words, what is the worst-case scenario as far as:

1. The number of years you will have to pay premiums

2. The amount of those premiums and how they might increase over the years

3. How low the benefits could drop.

Cost of dropping a policy early

Some insurance policies build up a "cash value" for you. You should find out what would be left of that cash value if you dropped a policy after 1, 5, 10, or 20 years.

39.

Buying the right amount and kind of life insurance

To determine the right amount and kind of life insurance you need, first analyze your purpose in buying the policy (see also pages 115 and 116).

For a policy that is taken out to help support a spouse and/or children, you should go through the following four steps with your life insurance agent, financial advisor, and/or attorney to determine the right amount of life insurance.

Step one: calculate your net worth

This involves looking at what you have and what you owe. Be realistic in adding up your assets and subtracting your liabilities (the result is your *net worth*).

Savings accounts, life insurance, retirement plans, and stocks are assets that can provide ready cash for your estate. If you are married, calculate what will be available, including life insurance, in the event of (1) your death, (2) your spouse's death, and (3) both of your deaths. For other assets such as real estate (that your children won't be living in), estimate the sales price of your assets after you're gone.

As for your liabilities, identify when large payments on debts will be due. In particular, are there regular mortgage payments on your house or investment property that are spread out evenly over 15 or 30 years or is there a balloon (i.e., large) payment that's due next year or in five years?

Step two: add up death-related costs and expenses

To do this, subtract from your net worth the expected death tax, income tax, attorney's fees, executor's (or trustee's) fees, and other death-related costs (such as funeral expenses).

Step three: determine the future needs of your children and/or spouse

This entails looking at your children's (and possibly your spouse's) circumstances. How much you want to have on hand for small children can be a very different story compared to grown children who are financially comfortable on their own. Also, you may have one or more children who have special disabilities that require additional resources.

What standard of living do you want your spouse or children to have? Do you want your children to be able to attend private school as a youngster as well as a private college as an adult? What about money for their graduate studies, too?

Where will your young children be living if you're not a-round? Will the people you're naming as their guardians need to add on to their house to have your children live there, too? Are you able to provide for that?

Step four: putting it all together to determine your insurance requirements

This step requires that you take all of the information from the first three steps and work backwards to come up with the necessary amount to leave for your children and/or spouse.

Begin by estimating the future income from your assets. Since we don't know what the future holds in the economy, you'll probably want to see results from different growth (e.g., 4%,

6%, 8%, and 10%) and inflation rates (e.g., 3%, 4%, 6%, and 8%).

Next, you should estimate how much your spouse and children will need per year (such as $10,000 for one child and $15,000 for another child) and build in an inflation factor for these expenses, too. Consider how much your family will be receiving from Social Security for survivors benefits.

Once you calculate the expected income and expenses over the years, you'll be able to see how long your money will last. Will your money be gone before all of your children are age 21? Age 18? Age 12?

The last decision is whether you want some money left over to give to your children after they attain a certain age (for example, age 21).

Use these four steps and make any necessary adjustments to calculate the sum of money you'll need to have on hand to provide for your family.

Rule of thumb for amount of coverage

A rule of thumb is to insure for five to eight times your annual salary in taking care of young children. If you have many children and just two thumbs, this rule may be too expensive to follow.

Do you want the IRS as a beneficiary on your life insurance?

You should remember that some of the insurance proceeds may go to the IRS instead of to your family, depending upon the size of your estate and the way you own life insurance. Talk to your attorney (and see page 124) about ways to insure that life insurance passes to your family free of federal death tax.

Types of policies and uses

Once you decide how much life insurance you need, the next step is to decide on the right kind of insurance for you.

There are two main types of life insurance: *cash value* (which includes whole life insurance) and *term*. There are variations of each type of policy and some policies combine both types of insurance within one policy package.

Since term insurance is more affordable and you may need considerable life insurance ($500,000 to $1,000,000 if you have young kids), you'll usually buy term insurance. A good cash value life insurance policy, however, is not one you'll regret having down the road.

Term insurance

Term insurance is the easier one to understand. Term insurance is like renting insurance—as long as you pay your premium, a death benefit will be paid. You don't own anything with term insurance. If you stop paying the premium, you walk away with nothing and no death benefit is payable.

If you are getting term insurance, purchase an annual renewable term policy so you don't have to pass physical exams each year to keep the policy as long as you want it.

Term insurance is more appropriate for shorter-term needs. For example, if you have children who are college-age or younger, you might want to be sure that there is enough money to educate them or to provide for them to age 18 or 21.

One mistake that is often made in families where both spouses work is the assumption that the kids will be able to get by, if they have to, on the income of one spouse. Well, what happens to that theory if both spouses pass away in a car accident? It's no fun thinking about the terrible possibilities that are out there, but part of the responsibility of being a parent is to make sure children are provided for in any eventuality. So, consider insuring each spouse.

Term insurance premium costs are initially lower than cash value life insurance but they may increase rapidly as one gets older (since the risk of dying increases over time, too).

You can have term insurance and at the same time keep premiums at the same level rate by purchasing *level premium term insurance*. With this type of insurance, the premium stays at the same cost for a specified period of time, such as 10 years, 15 years, or 20 years.

Since cost is a factor, always determine the cost of term insurance (including level term insurance) before making your decision.

Cash value (and whole life) life insurance

Cash value life insurance is a combination of term insurance (it provides a death benefit) with a tax-deferred investment component. A common type of cash value life insurance is whole life insurance.

Cash value life insurance is generally intended to be lifelong insurance (rather than for a shorter term) and it costs more than term insurance in the earlier years.

There are many variations of cash value life insurance. They range from conservative to more risky in their operation and effect. In general, all types of cash value life policies allow for tax-deferred growth and non-taxable distributions through loans and withdrawals.

Special life insurance for married couples

Spouses can also purchase permanent insurance that pays on the first death. This type of policy, often called *first-to-die insurance*, can be used for a family where both spouses work and the survivor would need insurance to replace the income of the spouse who died.

There's another kind of policy, often called *second-to-die insurance*, that may be of more interest to your parents. It is commonly used to replenish an estate for death taxes that are due on the death of the second spouse. This type of policy is generally less expensive than two separate policies because it is covering the lives of two people but the insurance company is paying off only one time, and only after two insureds have passed away. See page 124 on ways to eliminate death tax on life insurance.

Get a sound company

As with any insurance, make sure the insurance company is rated highly by A.M. Best, Moody's, Standard & Poor's, Weiss Research and Duff & Phelps.

You could reduce your risk on any sizeable amount of insurance by using two companies rather than one. You'll need to compare any extra cost with the comfort you'll receive splitting the coverage between two companies.

Since life insurance is a long-term investment, you'll need a well established and financially sound company when the time comes to collect proceeds.

40.

Life insurance do's and don'ts

Although state laws generally protect life insurance proceeds from creditors, there is one way that the proceeds will definitely get thrown in the pot and probably be subject to the claims of creditors: if one's estate is named as the beneficiary on a life insurance policy, then the proceeds may not only have to go through probate unnecessarily but they also can be claimed by creditors, justly or unjustly.

Life insurance money may also end up in your probate estate if all of the beneficiaries you name on the designation form fail to survive you. If you named your parents as the primary and backup beneficiaries on a policy and they both pass away before you, the life insurance proceeds would probably end up in your probate estate. Instead, if you had updated your beneficiary designations, the proceeds could have been paid quickly and correctly to the beneficiaries you had in mind without having to go through probate. (See page 138 for a further discussion of probate).

So, talk to your attorney about how to fill out your beneficiary designations forms. The forms may look insignificant but the choice of a few words can affect generations.

Also, don't assume that life insurance will escape death tax. You need to take special steps as described on page 124.

41.

Ways to avoid
death tax on life insurance

In general, each person can bequeath up to $625,000 (the *federal death tax exemption* limit) in 1998 with no federal death tax (U.S. citizen spouses can leave an unlimited amount to each other with no death tax until both spouses are gone). By the year 2006, the $625,000 figure will reach $1,000,000.

Most people think you don't count life insurance when you are determining whether federal death tax is due. Actually, it depends. If life insurance pushes you over the federal death tax exemption limit (or if you're already above that amount), your estate could land in the taxing zone, a zone that starts at least the 37% rate and goes up from there.

What this means is that a good portion or even a majority of the insurance policy proceeds on your death could go to *Uncle Sam* rather than to your real family. If you don't do advance planning, you might as well name Uncle Sam on the beneficiary designation form.

There are two ways, however, to keep the insurance proceeds from being taxable for death tax purposes: either have an *irrevocable life insurance trust* (i.e., a trust that cannot be changed) or have your children own, apply for, and pay for the policy.

Ask your attorney whether a life insurance trust or direct ownership (and premium payments) by your children makes sense for you. The time to ask about all of this is before you apply for a policy although certain steps can be taken to utilize existing policies, too.

42.

The right and wrong way
to name beneficiaries

Beneficiary designations generally override your will or trust.

If the beneficiaries under your will or trust differ from those selected in other designations (e.g., life insurance, retirement plan, and IRA), you should make it clear in your will or trust that this has been done intentionally. This will avoid potentially costly fights and help keep family harmony. Also, consider the income tax and death tax ramifications resulting from beneficiary designations (see pages 80 and 81).

Three overlooked issues in beneficiary designations

The first issue involves the consequences of failing to specify a secondary or contingent beneficiary on a beneficiary form. If your primary beneficiary does not survive you, that can mean in many cases that the benefits will be paid to your estate.

There are two main problems with benefits going into your estate. First, the benefits become subject to attorney's and executor's fees and delays that might otherwise have been avoided. Second, if the benefits are paid to your estate, an asset that may have been exempt from creditors' claims might well be converted to one that could be taken by creditors.

The second overlooked issue in beneficiary designations involves failing to specify what will happen to the benefits earmarked for a child if the child does not outlive you but leaves a child (your grandchild) who does survive you. Your beneficiary designation can be worded to deal with this possibility.

The third issue concerns whether you've named individual(s) or a trust on your beneficiary designation. Whom you name as beneficiaries can determine how long income tax may be postponed on certain retirement benefits. Your attorney and tax advisor can tell whether this tax postponement possibility is available to you.

Keep designations current

Always keep your beneficiary designations up to date to reflect your current intent and do so with the assistance of legal advice to make sure the designation works with, and not against, your estate plan.

43.

What to look for in a disability insurance policy

Disability policies are not all the same. They can vary widely in cost and benefits. In general, there are two benefits from purchasing a policy while you are younger: (1) the cost is lower and (2) you are still insurable and not subject to a health condition that may disqualify you from coverage.

When you find a policy, see how it handles at least the following seven items:

1. Check if the benefits are payable for life (or at least until age 65) instead of a maximum period such as for five years. Keep in mind that normal retirement age for your age group is age 67—it's not age 65 (and it will probably be at least age 70 by the time you retire).

2. See if the benefits *(a)* increase with inflation (i.e., is there a "cost-of-living adjustment" or "COLA"?) or *(b)* give you options to increase coverage over time without the requirement of a physical examination rather than just staying a fixed dollar amount during the life of the policy.

3. Review the definition of the term *disability* in the policy to see if benefits will be paid if you can't work in your *current occupation* or only if you can't do *any kind of work*.

4. Calculate how long you can afford to wait before the benefits become payable—one month, three months, one year. The longer the waiting period, the lower the

premium. Don't be overly optimistic about your ability to survive financially while you are disabled. A three-month waiting period might be realistic for you.

5. Since partial disabilities are not uncommon, check to see if partial disability benefits are included without your having to be totally disabled.

6. See whether premiums are waived (excused) if you are disabled.

7. Read the policy to be sure you understand the exclusions under the policy.

Finally, see if your policy can be converted into a long-term care policy at retirement age irrespective of your medical condition is at that time.

Who should pay the premiums?

If you become disabled and receive benefits under a disability insurance policy, those benefits may or may not be free of income tax. Having income-tax free benefits could be extremely important to you while you are disabled.

In general, if you personally pay the insurance premiums as compared to a company paying the premiums, the benefits will be income-tax free to you. If, instead, your employer pays the premiums, then the benefits will be subject to income tax. Be sure to review this topic with your disability insurance agent, accountant, and attorney.

44.

How to plan for rainy days: umbrella insurance

This is not a society where people are shy about suing.

The usual amount of car insurance doesn't protect you against the major losses that can easily occur.

One relatively inexpensive solution is to have *umbrella insurance* on top of your regular car and home liability insurance. This kind of insurance starts paying when your other insurance coverage is exhausted. You may be able to get up to $1 million, $2 million or more of coverage for far less than you think.

Ask your liability insurance agent about umbrella insurance. That way you may not get soaked when a bit of rain pours into your life.

WILLS & TRUSTS

45.

Why have a will or living trust?

If you don't sign a will, your state will write one for you when you're gone. The state will say who inherits from you, who raises your children, when your children will get total control of any inheritance (e.g., a child may receive a lump-sum inheritance at age eighteen), produce the worst death tax and income tax result for your successors and result in a greater amount of legal and other court-related fees if a probate (see page 138) is required.

With a properly drafted will and/or trust (and coordinated steps on beneficiary designations and title to assets), you will be in control of the ultimate destination of your assets, making sure the right persons are taking care of your children and maybe saving death taxes for your loved ones.

For most people, the magic number will be at least $625,000 as to whether there will be any federal death tax. For estates below that size, no federal death tax should be due for deaths occurring in 1998. The 1997 tax act is gradually increasing the $625,000 exempt amount each year to get up to $1,000,000 for deaths in the year 2006 or later. U.S. citizen spouses can leave an unlimited amount to each other with no death tax until both spouses are gone.

Depending upon how a husband and wife set up their wills and/or living trusts and ownership of assets, they could each potentially have a $625,000 exemption in 1998 (and up to $1,000,000 in the year 2006) or a total $1,250,000 million exemption in 1998 (and up to $2,000,000 in the year 2006) for the family.

Let's look at how this could work for a couple worth $625,000 each for a total of $1,250,000 together. This number is not far-fetched for many couples when you realize that life insurance (unless special steps are taken in advance—see page 124) and retirement plan benefits are part of the equation.

$245,000 in unnecessary death tax

If one spouse worth $625,000 leaves all of his or her assets outright to the surviving spouse (worth $625,000, too), then the survivor will be worth $1,250,000 at the time of his or her death. If the surviving spouse can shield $625,000 from death tax (upon dying in 1998), then the remaining $625,000 will be taxed. The federal death tax in this scenario would be $245,000. There is a way to keep that $245,000 within the family instead of making this donation to the IRS.

Death tax savings trust

This $245,000 federal death tax could go down to zero on the $1,250,000 in assets if the first spouse to die had set up a will or trust with a *death tax saving trust* (sometimes called a *B trust, credit shelter trust* or *exemption trust*). The reason is that assets of the first to die in a properly drafted death tax saving trust will not be counted as being owned by the surviving spouse. The assets of the first to die would be shielded from death tax by the $625,000 exemption permitted for the first to die (this exemption goes up each year from $625,000 in 1998 to $1,000,000 in the year 2006).

With a death tax saving trust in a will or trust, the surviving spouse could be the beneficiary of the trust and, in some cases, be the trustee (manager) of the trust as well. Your attorney can explain how this type of trust works.

Ask your attorney if there will be state inheritance tax and/or federal and state income tax even if there is no federal death tax.

Maybe the best will to leave to your children

It's well and good to be fortunate enough to leave a monetary inheritance to your children.

But one of the greatest gifts you can give to your child or children does not have a monetary value—it has an ethical value. When all is said and done, most of us want ourselves and our children to be good people who make the world a better place.

We don't often take the time to put on paper what values we hold as our ideals. But an "ethical will" lets you do just that.

Ethical wills date back to biblical times. An ethical will does not have a set format. If you want further direction, there are books that provide examples of ethical wills.

An ethical will tells your children the values you hold deepest, the most important lessons you've learned in life, your favorite sayings, special family expressions and the religious or secular writings you hold dearest to your heart. You might tell of mistakes you've made and, sometimes, even ask for forgiveness. This might be the time to finish unfinished business (the lawyer in me does ask that you show your ethical will to your attorney so that this separate document does not contain material that might upset the apple cart of your monetary estate plan).

You can put your ethical will in writing or on a videotape with a camcorder.

Tell your children what you value the most. What a tragedy it would be if you pass on without sharing with them what is most important to you.

46.

Guardian angels for your children when you're not around

First off, your will should name guardians for your minor children. There are two types of guardians.

Guardian of the person

Talk to your attorney about naming a personal guardian for your minor children. This "guardian of the person" will be the one in charge of raising your children. The guardian of the person makes the decisions about your children's education, religious training (or lack of training) and other matters that you would handle as a parent. This is not a job about managing money for your minor children. You are entrusting someone to instill values in your children and ensure their well-being.

When you provide your choices to your attorney, list as many qualified people as possible since you do not know who will be willing and able to serve when the time arises. Before your will is completed, you should ask your desired guardians if they'll serve on your behalf and whether they have any special conditions or requests.

One way to evaluate a potential guardian is to take a good look at how they're raising their own children.

Depending upon the age and maturity of your children (and their ability to discuss the subject of your deaths), you might ask them their opinion about the choices you have in mind.

A trickier issue is how you select relatives from each (or neither) side of your family and in what order. The overriding factor should be the best interests of your children, not whether someone's feelings will be hurt if they are way down or even off your list of potential guardians.

Guardian of the estate

If any assets pass from you or from anyone else directly to your minor children, someone needs to manage the assets until the children become adults. That someone is called a "guardian of the estate." An example of how assets could pass directly to your children would be if you named your young children as the beneficiaries on your life insurance policy.

Who should be the guardian of the estate? Usually it's the same person you've named as executor or trustee. The guardian of the estate performs a similar job of managing your children's assets.

Who's the right choice for these money-managing jobs? Above all, you want someone who's honest and who has good common sense. A guardian of the estate or executor or trustee does not need to be a financial whiz. However, your representative should be a prudent person who knows when to ask for financial, tax or legal advice and does so. Another factor to keep in mind is whether your choice has any conflict of interest. Will your representative inherit assets that are not paid out to other beneficiaries?

Try to use trusts to avoid having assets pass directly to minor children and ending up in a "guardianship." Trusts can reduce court involvement, attorneys fees and court costs and keep an 18-year old child from receiving a lump sum guardianship payment of $250,000 in life insurance proceeds on an eighteenth birthday. That lump sum payment might mean the end of a college education and the beginning of an around-the-world spending spree.

47.

Probate and how to avoid it

Probate is the court process by which your assets are transferred from you (actually from your estate) to your successors after you die. Not all of your assets have to go through probate (talk to your attorney about the ways to avoid probate, even without a living trust). The bad news with probate is that the attorney's and executor's fees are usually quite costly (often two to five percent for the attorney and a similar amount for your executor) and it can take considerable time (usually a year or so) to complete the transfer of your assets to your successors.

Probate takes place after your death. During the process, your assets are located and valued, your creditors and death taxes are paid and, at the end, distribution is made to your successors.

A living trust may avoid probate where a will won't. A living trust is a legal document spelling out the management and distribution of your assets while you are alive and after you die. Once you pass away, a living trust is like a will in that it says who gets what and when.

A living trust is not for everyone. You need to review your situation with your attorney to see whether a living trust is right for you. Usually the older and wealthier you are, the more your family can benefit from a living trust.

Also see pages 125 and 126 regarding beneficiary designations and avoiding probate.

MAKING MONEY FROM YOUR PAPERWORK

48.

How financial records can save you taxes on your house

Having organized financial records can save you income taxes when you sell your house. Too many people are going to make a mistake and stop keeping track of home improvements thinking the $250,000/$500,000 federal exclusions under the 1997 tax act will eliminate the need to keep records.

Selling your house

You may owe income tax when you sell your house.

When you sell your house, income tax may be due on the gain above your original cost plus improvements. You need to have organized records to keep track of the improvements that may reduce the income tax due on a sale. You should set up a separate file that makes it easy to store and locate the invoices and checks to substantiate the improvements made to your house.

Although there are ways to avoid paying federal income tax if you sell your house, at some point you may have to pay the piper. (See page 45 on how the gain may not be taxed at all.)

There are three reasons to still keep track of improvements even with the 1997 federal law. First, the new tax law is a federal law, not a state law. Your state may have different rules. Even if your state adopts a law just like the federal law, you may move to a new state (or to a vacation home there) that has different rules. Second, there may be great inflation in the coming years so that the $250,000/$500,000

THE GENERATION X MONEY BOOK

exclusions will not cover the gain over the coming decades. Third, the federal income tax rules may change over time.

49.

How financial records can save you taxes on stocks and mutual funds

If you invest in stocks or mutual funds, from time to time you'll want or need to sell shares to buy a house, make a downpayment on a house, pay for your children's college education, or take a needed vacation.

Stocks or mutual funds may be in a tax-deferred investment (e.g., a traditional IRA) that will grow income-tax free (including gains on sale) until distributions are taken out.

However, you may own such stocks or funds just in your own name and sales would be subject to income tax. You may be able to reduce or eliminate the income tax on such a sale of stock or mutual fund share if you have organized records.

If an investment has gone up in value since you purchased it, you will owe income tax on the sale of that investment. Very often you will have purchased additional shares over time. Will you owe income tax if some of the investment has gone up and some has gone down in value since you purchased it?

With organized records, you could direct the sale of those portions of your stock or mutual fund shares that produced the lowest income tax due.

How to avoid paying extra, unnecessary income tax

If you invest in a mutual fund and reinvest the dividends rather than take them out, organized records may allow you to reduce the gain upon a sale.

Suppose you put $1,000 into a fund in your personal name (and outside of any retirement plan or IRA) and over the years you received $300 in dividends, which were reinvested in the fund. You now have $1,300 invested. When you decide to sell your interest in the fund for $2,000, good records will show that you have $700 of gain ($2,000 less $1,300) not $1,000 of gain ($2,000 less $1,000) since the reinvested dividends were previously taxed.

Tracking down your stock cost basis

You may need assistance in figuring out how much you've paid for stock that you bought over time or through payroll deductions. The first place to look is your library and see if the Standard and Poor's Guide gives you enough information. If not, you might want to contact Prudential American Securities (1/626/795-5831, California) and for a fee they'll search for information you can use to reconstruct your purchase history.

50.

Finding lost treasures

Hundreds of billions of dollars in assets have been misplaced in the United States. This money is being held by the federal government, state government, insurance companies and banks. It's not surprising considering the way people move around the country, change their names, change their jobs, forget to send in change of address forms and fall prey to a fading memory as the years go by. Add to that the frenzied pace of company mergers and corporate name changes and you have a recipe for lost treasure.

Fortunately, it's getting easier to track down lost assets. A good starting point is the National Association of Unclaimed Property Administrators. You can go to their Website (http://www.intersurf.com/~naupa/). You can also check out lists put out by states on their Internet sites. When in doubt, check everywhere including life insurance companies and government pension plans. Old checkbook registers and income tax returns are good sources to help locate lost assets.

U.S. Savings Bonds

Too many people do not keep track of their U.S. Savings Bonds maturity dates. Bonds don't pay interest forever so don't let yours be among those that have stopped earning interest. Also see pages 98 and 99 for resource information on Savings Bonds.

Finding vital records

If you need to locate a certified copy of a birth, death, marriage or divorce certificate, get a copy of the U.S. Department of Health and Human Services' booklet "Where to Write for Vital Records."

You can order the booklet by calling 1/719/948-4000 or see it on-line at http://www.pueblo.gsa.gov/misc.htm.

APPENDIX

Appendix

*Examples of Social Security Disability
and Survivors benefits*

Disability benefit examples

For these examples of monthly Social Security disability
benefits, assume you were age 25 in 1997, became disabled in
1997 and had steady lifetime earnings (the following survivors
benefit examples assume you passed away in 1997):

Your 1996 earnings	Your monthly benefit	Monthly benefit for you, your spouse, and child
$20,000	$ 797	$1,195
30,000	1,063	1,595
40,000	1,229	1,844
50,000	1,354	2,032
62,700	1,508	2,262

or more (See Note 1 below)

The accuracy of these estimates and the survivors benefits
below depends on the pattern of your earnings in prior years.

Note 1: Assumes earnings were equal to or greater than the
OASDI wage base from age 22 through 1996.

Survivors benefit examples

Your 1996 earnings	Monthly benefit for your spouse and one child	Monthly benefit for your spouse and two children
$20,000	$1,194	$1,459
30,000	1,594	1,874
40,000	1,844	2,152
50,000	2,032	2,371
62,700	2,240	2,614
or more (See Note 1 above)		

Great Way to Search the Internet

If you want to minimize frustration in searching the Internet for information, check out *Inference Find*.

The best way I've found to locate information, Web sites or resources is *Inference Find* (http://www.inference.com/ifind/).

Inference Find is a fast Internet search tool that combines the results of many search engines and groups the results in understandable categories. Just call up the site, type in your search request and seven seconds later, you can view the organized results on your screen.

Software and Internet Sites of Interest

Software to do retirement planning

Before you purchase software to do retirement planning, please check whether (1) the software has been updated for the latest federal tax legislation, (2) you're purchasing the latest version of the program and (3) your computer has enough power and speed to make using the program enjoyable and rewarding.

Besides the programs listed below, you can also do on-line calculations on some of the Internet sites listed on pages 152 and 153.

- *Vanguard Retirement Planner*
  Call 1/800/876-1840. The program is inexpensive, easy to use and uses graphics very effectively.

- *Quicken Deluxe for Windows (by Intuit)*
  Call 1/800/224-0991. Ask about the *Financial Planner*.

On-line financial information (Web site addresses do change.)

College cost calculations and sources of financial aid
  http://finaid.org/
  http://www.vanguard.com

Education about basic investment information:
  http://www.aaii.org

Financial information
  http://www.americanexpress.com/direct
  http://www.cnnfn.com/quickenonfn/
  http://www.smartmoney.com

Home loans
 http://www.countrywide.com
 http://QuickenMortgage.com

Internal Revenue Service
 http://www.irs.gov

IRA calculations: Roth IRA vs. traditional IRA
 Vanguard IRA Worksheet on their Internet Web site
 (http://www.vanguard.com)

Pension benefits
 http://www.dol.gov/dol/pwba/welcome.html

Retirement planning
 http://www.americanexpress.com/direct (select Financial
  Tools, then select Retirement Savings)
 http://quicken.excite.com (under Retirement, select Getting
  Started and then select Build Your Plan)
 http://www.fidelity.com (select Personal Investing, then select
  Retirement Investing, then select Retirement
  Toolkit and then select Retirement Planning
  Calculator)
 http://working4u.scudder.com
 http://www.vanguard.com (select Planning Center, then
  select Retirement Resource Center, then select
  Planning for Retirement, then select How Much
  Should You Save for Retirement)
Small business
 http://www.americanexpress.com/smallbusiness
 http://www.business.gov
 http://www.visa.com/smallbiz

Social Security
 http://www.ssa.gov

Books Worth Considering

The Privacy Rights Handbook: How To Take Control of Your Personal Information by Beth Givens and The Privacy Rights Clearinghouse (Avon Books).

"It's vital to get *The Privacy Rights Handbook* to the millions of Americans who are unaware of how 'invisible hands' manipulate their daily life."
— Ralph Nader (from the Foreword)

The book is available in bookstores or it may be purchased directly from the Privacy Rights Clearinghouse (1/619/298-3396, California).

A Parent's (and Grandparent's) Guide to Wills & Trusts by Don Silver (Adams-Hall Publishing).

"Excellent book. It is clear. It is concise. It is clever."
— *Los Angeles Times*

The book is available in bookstores or it may be purchased directly from Adams-Hall Publishing (1/800/888-4452, California).

Index

Index

Disability benefits
part-time work and, 60-62
Social Security as source of,
28-29, 60-62, 149
Disability insurance, 127-128
Disinheritance
joint tenancy and, 77-79
Distributions from retirement
plans. *See* Retirement plans
Diversify investments, 22, 32
Divorce, 87-88
effect on college education
fund, 99
ex-spouse inheriting and, 91-
92
Social Security benefits
affected by, 76, 91
Domicile, 72

E

Education IRA, 100-101, 104
Ethical wills, 135

F

FDIC, 40
Fidelity
Web site, 153
Financial advisor
selecting, 13, 35-37
401(k) plan
beneficiary designations and,
125-126
benefits and, 21, 32
conduit IRA and, 23
dangers in borrowing against,
22
death tax and, 81
features of, 20, 21-23
income tax on inheritance of,
80
reducing taxes and, 21-22
Roth IRA and, 11, 12, 16-20,
21

Funeral arrangements, 83-84

G

Gifts
for college education, 106-107
for medical bills, 106
grandparents and college
education, 106
reducing death tax with, 107
Goals, financial, 9, 32
Guardians, 136-137

H

Health matters, 57, 71, 75-76, 82-
83, 91
Health power of attorney, 82-83
Home equity loan, 105
dangers and, 10
deducting interest and, 10, 53-
54
Home offices, 61-63
Homeschooling, 60-63
Hope Credits, 101-102
House. *See* Real estate

I

Incapacity
disability insurance and, 127-
128
health power of attorney and,
82-83
living trusts and, 77-79, 82-83
living will and, 82-83
Social Security benefits and,
149
Income tax. *See also* Capital gain
tax, Tax-deferral and Tax-
free income
beneficiary designations and,
81, 125-126

L

Life insurance
 accelerated death benefits and, 64
 beneficiary designations and, 125-126
 both spouses working and, 120-121
 college education savings and, 104
 death tax and, 87-88, 124
 income tax free, 64
 life insurance trusts and, 124
 need for, 115-116
 Social Security survivors benefits and, 150
 soundness of companies and, 122
 term, 120-121
 types, 120-121
 viatical settlements and, 64
 whole life, 121-122
Life support. See Health power of attorney; Living will
Living trusts
 avoiding probate and, 138
 incapacity and, 82-83
 joint tenancy compared to, 77-79
Living will, 82-83
Loans. See also Mortgage
Long-term care. See Nursing home expenses.
Lost assets, 145-146
 Web site, 145, 146

M

Marital agreement
 marriage and liabilities with, 75-76
 moving and validity of, 70
Marriage (and Remarriage)

beneficiary designations and, 93-94, 125-126
college aid and, 88, 90
death taxes and, 81
divorce and, 76, 87-88, 91
life insurance for spouse in, 115, 117-124
joint tenancy and, 77-79, 87
moving and, 72
nursing home care expenses and, 72, 75-76
real estate and, 45
Social Security benefits and, 87-88
title to assets and, 87-88
trust and, 87-88, 93-94, 133-135
will and, 87-88, 93-94, 133-135
Mortgage
 credit report and, 47, 66
 dangers, 9-11, 46
 deducting interest and, 9-11, 45
 payment plans, 48-52
 reducing interest paid on, 11, 47, 48-52
 Web sites, 153
Moving
 health insurance and, 71
 income tax and, 69
 marital agreement and, 70
 nursing home costs and, 72
 purchasing residence and, 45, 53, 72
 trusts and, 69-70
 wills and, 69-70
Mutual funds, 15, 19
 diversify, 22, 32, 40
 safety, 40
 income tax and, 15-20

N

National Association of Financial Aid Administrators, 105
 Web site, 105

R

Rates of return
  credit card interest and, 9-11
  for bonds, historically, 33
  for stocks, historically, 5, 33
Real estate. *See* Mortgage
  borrowing against, 10, 11, 47,
      48-52, 53
  buying or renting, 45-47
  death taxes and, 81
  home equity loan on, 10, 53,
      54
  home offices, 61-63
  income tax, 45-46, 141-142
  joint tenancy and, 77-79
  refinancing, 10, 11, 53, 54
  renting or buying, 45-47
  residence and saving income
      tax, 45-46
  saving income tax and, 45-46
  selling, 45, 141-142
Record-keeping, 59, 141-146
Refinancing, 10, 11, 53
Remarriage. *See* Marriage
Retirement plans. *See* also IRA
      and Roth IRA
  bankruptcy and, 41
  beneficiary designations, 125-
      126
  death taxes and, 81
  defined benefit plans, 24-27
  distributions, 17, 24-27, 38-39,
      75, 89, 93
  401(k) plan, 21-23
  income tax on inheritance
      and, 80
  IRA rollovers and, 18, 22-23
  limits on FDIC insurance, 40
  marriage and, 75, 89, 93, 125
  mistakes and, 24-25
  National Center for
      Retirement Benefits, Inc.,
      25
  reducing income tax, 15-20,

  22-23, 38-39
  remarriage and, 75, 89, 93
  summary plan descriptions
      and, 25-27
  waiver, 75, 89, 93
  withdrawals, 15-20, 21-22, 38-
      39, 126
Retirement saving
  examples of savings
      requirements, 5, 6-8, 11
  401(k) plan and, 21
  right amount of, 11, 12-14
  when to start saving, 5, 6-8,
      11, 12-14, 21, 34
Risk
  assessing comfort level of, 34
  avoiding, 34
Rollover. *See* also Retirement
      plans
  consider avoiding, 22-23
  Roth IRA, 18
Roth IRA, 11, 12, 16-20, 21 101,
      103, 106

S

Safe deposit box
  funeral arrangements and, 83-
      84
Saving
  by record keeping, 141-146
  by reducing death tax, 93-95,
      124, 133-135
  by reducing debt expenses,
      9-11
  by reducing income tax, 6, 10,
      11, 15-20, 38-39, 45, 53, 54,
      62-63, 64, 69, 80, 81, 87, 88,
      91, 98-99, 100-103, 119, 122,
      141-144
  by reducing mortgage interest,
      48-52
  examples of, 5, 6-7, 12
  retirement, 6-8, 9-11, 12-14, 15-
      20, 21-23

Scudder
  Web site, 153
Second income, 60-63
Simplification, 59
Small business
  Web sites, 153
Smartmoney Web site, 152
Social Security
  avoiding divorce and, 91
  children's benefits under, 28-
    29, 149-150
  correcting mistakes in benefits
    for, 30
  disability benefits, 28-29, 60-
    62, 149
  divorce and 76, 91, 92
  form for benefits and earnings
    under, 29
  marriage and, 91
  part-time work and, 60-62
  remarriage and, 91-92
  Request for Earnings and
    Benefit Estimate Statement,
    29
  survivors benefits and, 28-
    29, 60-62, 150
  Web site, 31, 153
Software for retirement planning,
  152-153
Stepped-up basis and income tax,
  18-19
Stocks
  saving income tax on, 15-20,
    143-145
Summary plan description
  items included in, 25-26

T

Tax Act of 1997. *See* Taxpayer
  Relief Act of 1997
Tax deductions
  home equity loans and, 11
  non-deductible interest, 11

Tax-deferral
  beneficiary designations and,
    125-126
  cash value life insurance and,
    121
  investments, 6, 16
  retirement plans, 6, 16-23
Taxes. *See* Death tax; Income tax
Tax-free income
  accelerated death benefits and,
    64
  disability insurance as, 127-
    128
  life insurance and, 64
  real estate, 45, 141-143
  Roth IRA, 11, 12, 16-20, 21,
    101, 103, 106
Taxpayer Relief Act of 1997, 16,
  45, 88, 91, 100
Terminal illness
  funeral arrangements and, 83-
    84
  health power of attorney and,
    82-83
  life insurance and, 64
  living will and, 82-83
Term life insurance, 120-121
Trusts
  beneficiary designations and,
    39, 125-126, 133-134
  death tax and, 81
  401(k) plan and, 23
  joint tenancy and, 77-79, 87-88
  life insurance, 124
  living trusts, 138
  marriage and, 75-76, 87-88
  moving and, 69-70
  real estate and, 45
  remarriage and, 75-76
  will and, 87-88
Tuition prepayment plans and
  college education, 103-104

Order Form

(Photocopy this page)

	Qty.	Total

THE GENERATION X MONEY BOOK:
Achieving Security and Independence by Don Silver
176 pages $14.95 plus 5¢ s/h = **$15 per book**   ____ $_____

    Sales tax for California residents $1.23 per book $_____

A PARENT'S GUIDE TO WILLS & TRUSTS (For Grandparents, Too) by Don Silver

Los Angeles Times: "Excellent book. It is clear.
It is concise. It is clever."
256 pages $11.95 plus 5¢ s/h = **$12 per book**   ____ $_____

    Sales tax for California residents 99¢ per book $_____

(FOR QUANTITY DISCOUNTS, CALL 1/800-888-4452) Total $_____

PAYMENT PREFERENCE:
    By check, payable to Adams-Hall Publishing or
    By credit card: Visa ___   MasterCard ___
                 Discover ___   American Express ___

ACCOUNT NUMBER:_____ EXPIRATION DATE:_____

NAME ON CARD:_____
                 (PLEASE PRINT CLEARLY)

      SIGNATURE:_____

PLEASE PRINT:

NAME_____

MAILING ADDRESS _____

CITY/STATE/ZIP CODE_____

DAYTIME TELEPHONE_____

Mail to: Adams-Hall Publishing, PO Box 491002, Dept. GX,
    Los Angeles, CA 90049 or call 1/800-888-4452